HEALING YOUR
GRIEVING HEART
AFTER A MILITARY DEATH

Also by Alan Wolfelt

The Depression of Grief:
Coping With Your Sadness and Knowing When to Get Help

Healing A Friend's Grieving Heart:
100 Practical Ideas for Helping Someone You Love Through Loss

Healing Your Grieving Heart: 100 Practical Ideas

Healing Your Traumatized Heart:
100 Practical Ideas After Someone You Love Dies a Sudden, Violent Death

The Journey Through Grief:
Reflections on Healing

The Mourner's Book of Courage:
30 Days of Encouragement

The PTSD Solution:
The Truth About Your Symptoms and How to Heal

Understanding Your Grief:
Ten Essential Touchstones for Finding Hope and Healing Your Heart

Understanding Your Suicide Grief:
Ten Essential Touchstones for Finding Hope and Healing Your Heart

*Companion Press is dedicated to the education
and support of both the bereaved and bereavement
caregivers. We believe that those who companion
the bereaved by walking with them as they journey
in grief have a wondrous opportunity: to help others
embrace and grow through grief—and to lead
fuller, more deeply-lived lives themselves
because of this important ministry.*

Companion
P R E S S

For a complete catalog and ordering information, write or call:

Companion Press
The Center for Loss and Life Transition
3735 Broken Bow Road
Fort Collins, CO 80526
(970) 226-6050
www.centerforloss.com

HEALING YOUR GRIEVING HEART AFTER A MILITARY DEATH

•

100 PRACTICAL IDEAS FOR FAMILIES AND FRIENDS

•

BONNIE CARROLL
ALAN D. WOLFELT, PH.D.

Companion
PRESS

Fort Collins, Colorado

An imprint of the Center for Loss and Life Transition

Companion Press is an imprint of the Center for Loss and Life Transition, 3735 Broken Bow Road, Fort Collins, Colorado 80526.

Printed in the United States of America.

21 20 19 18 17 16 15   5 4 3 2 1

ISBN: 978-1-61722-234-4

In Gratitude

*To the military families who have allowed
us to companion them in the face of profound grief.
Thank you for inspiring us to create this resource.*

I have only slipped away into the next room...

I am I, and you are you...
Whatever we were to each other, that we are still.

Call me by the old familiar name.
Speak of me in the easy way which you always used.

Laugh as we always laughed at the little jokes that we enjoyed together.
Play, smile, think of me, pray for me.
Let my name be ever the household word that it always was.
Let it be spoken without an effort, without the ghost of a shadow upon it.

Life means all that it ever meant...

Why should I be out of mind because I am out of sight?
I am but waiting for you, for an interval,
somewhere very near,
just round the corner.

— Henry Scott Holland

CONTENTS

INTRODUCTION

"With the tears a Land hath shed
Their graves should ever be green."
— Thomas Bailey Aldrich

Someone you love served, and died, in the military. The unique nature of your loss colors so many aspects of your grief journey. In this little book, we hope to affirm your experience and offer you compassionate encouragement to mourn openly, honestly, and thoroughly so that the rest of your life—and your loved one's legacy—can be as full and as meaningful as possible.

While your grief can make you feel isolated, you are not alone. Over the course of American history, well over a million military members have died during their time of service. Hundreds of thousands have died in battle, most during the Civil War and World War II. In recent decades, hostile action has continued to claim the lives of thousands of service members, but even more have died as a result of accidents. Some die of illness during their service. Others take their own lives.

Regardless of the branch of service, the circumstances of the death, or your relationship to the person who died, if you are grieving in the aftermath of a military death, this book is for you.

Grieving a military death

It's true that the day your service member joined the military is the day you, too, joined the military—particularly if you are a close family member. The military is a world unto itself. It is an incredibly strong culture with its own rules, language, clothing, housing, and other conventions. And it is not only a tight-knit organization. It becomes an extension of family.

Your loved one's service branch likely took control in the initial days and weeks following the death. Many of you first learned of the death from the "knock on the door" by a casualty notification officer. After that were many other military protocols, including, often, a military funeral as well as ongoing discussions and paperwork about things like benefits and housing.

On the one hand, the military way of doing things may have provided you with a helpful structure in those early days. They may have held you up and helped you survive. We hope your military "family" surrounded you with support and care as they honored your loved one. On the other hand, the military way of doing and talking about things may have distanced you from the reality of what happened or made it feel like it was as much their loss as yours. Sometimes the power of the military culture, both immediately after a death and long into the future, can seem impersonal compared to survivors' unique thoughts and feelings.

The military has strong traditions of duty, honor, and country, emphasizing faithfulness and loyalty. Service members feel responsible for those they lead or serve shoulder-to-shoulder with. All these levels of loyalty are understandable and admirable. But when you become a family member or friend left behind, you might find yourself wondering if service to God, country, and colleague was really more important than loyalty to you. It is normal and natural for such questions to arise during your grief journey.

Then there is the outsider view of military deaths. Inside the military, we revere those who die while serving. Outside the military, people who do not understand or agree with military service or combat don't always respect military deaths, either. While picketing of funerals is an extreme and relatively rare example, unkind or misinformed remarks are more common.

What's more, military deaths are often very public deaths. They are on the TV news and in the newspapers. The person who died served his community, and therefore many community members grieve, discuss the death, attend the funeral, etc. They may peer into the grieving family's life for a time, shed a tear for the loss, feel gratitude for the deceased's service, and then go back to their lives. Yet the family is just emerging from the shock of the loss and beginning to feel the grief that will be with them forever. It is difficult to find a place of peace between the public honors and private grief. And sometimes to family and close friends, it can seem like the military, the country, and the community act as if they "own" the loss more than you do, and this can be hurtful and confusing.

Following military deaths that are not so public, such as by accident, suicide, or illness, there may be an even greater sense of disenfranchisement if the life of service is not honored in the same way that a combat death is recognized. The family experiences the same "knock on the door," the same folded flag, the same benefits and burial, but there isn't the public acknowledgment. When asked how their loved one died, these families may respond "in the military," which may prompt questions about combat or comments about war. This can make families feel that their loss is less heroic and somehow different, although they feel the same pain of loss.

For spouses who were living on a military installation, the death of the service member means they must move away, complicating the grief journey in a number of ways. It can be very difficult to leave the last house their loved one called "home," pack up all their belongings, including military uniforms and gear, and head to a new home that wasn't part of the family's plan. They may have to leave their best network of support—the military friends who had been "right there" to hug them, talk to them, and empathize with them in ways civilians can't. For children, the death often means they must leave their school and their friends and start over in a place where no one may know their parent or understand the life they have lived.

Another reason that grieving a military death is complicated and unique is that those who die are usually young and healthy. Whenever a young person dies for any reason, we struggle with the out-of-order nature of the death. Children aren't supposed to die before their parents. Parents aren't supposed to die before their own children are grown. Young people aren't supposed to die before they've had a chance to marry or to raise their own families. The typical robust physical health of military service members makes their deaths even more unbelievable and incongruous. After all, they must pass special fitness tests to join the Armed Forces, and they regularly receive training and continued physical exams and fitness testing to ensure they maintain the highest standards of health and well-being. Even when they go into combat, they are protected by state-of-the-art armor, and despite the risks, are equipped to survive. We may struggle to understand how such a young, healthy, trained, and protected person could die.

SUICIDE IN THE MILITARY

One of the leading causes of death in the military is suicide. Suicide is never simple. It is a complex "perfect storm" of factors that may include traumatic brain injury, combat fatigue, post-traumatic stress, previous life trauma, chronic pain, complications from medications, sleep deprivation, and life challenges. Your loved one did not stop loving you. He or she stopped the pain.

If your loved one died as a result of suicide, you are not alone. We invite you to contact the Tragedy Assistance Program for Survivors, or TAPS, at 800-959-8277. In addition to the services mentioned on page 5, TAPS also coordinates an annual National Military Suicide Survivor Seminar and Good Grief Camp, where hundreds of families gather to support one another and learn about other resources. Military suicide survivor support groups are also available through TAPS.

We also suggest that you read Dr. Wolfelt's book specifically for suicide survivors entitled *Understanding Your Suicide Grief: Ten Essential Touchstones for Finding Hope and Healing Your Heart*. It contains much more in-depth discussion and guidance for loved ones in the aftermath of a suicide. There is also a companion journal that can help you work through your grief, *The Understanding Your Suicide Grief Journal*.

And of course, the sudden and violent nature of many military deaths has a significant effect on the grief experience of survivors, too. Whenever we are exposed to a traumatic incident, whether we experience it ourselves, firsthand, or someone we love experiences it, we suffer some degree of post-traumatic stress.

Naturally, traumatized mourners often find themselves replaying and reconsidering the circumstances of the death. This is both normal and necessary. Such replay helps you begin to acknowledge the reality of the death and integrate it into your life. It is as if your mind needs to devote time and energy to comprehending the circumstances of the death before it can move on to confronting the fact that someone you love has died and will never be present to you again.

We will talk a little more about traumatic grief and post-traumatic stress later in this book, but for now, we just want to affirm that the way in which your loved one died is part of your grief experience. If you continue to suffer from disabling fear and anxiety and are having trouble functioning in your day-to-day life, please get help from a professional grief counselor. You deserve compassionate care. But many of you are traumatized without having full-blown post-traumatic stress. You may have anxiety and anger. You may think about the circumstances of the death a lot. You may be in great pain. But if you are still able to function in your daily life and interact lovingly with others, you may not have the actual disorder called PTSD. Still, you are traumatized and in need of special care and consideration, both from yourself and from others.

The traumatic nature of the death and your thoughts and feelings about it will color every aspect of your grief. It is part of your grief. But it is not the totality of your grief. Other factors that contribute to your grief include the nature of the relationship you had with the person who died, your unique personality, your religious and cultural backgrounds, your gender, your age, and your previous experiences with loss. Your grief is a complicated blend of thoughts and emotions, most of which stem from your love for the person who died. Over time you will come to find that your grief is as much or more about the life than it is about the death.

About TAPS

When someone dies while serving in the Armed Forces or in support of our nation's freedoms, those who love them and grieve their death have a special place where they can find comfort and care, hope and healing. TAPS helps family members and friends come together to remember the love, celebrate the life, and share the journey.

Since 1994, TAPS has been the home where military families gather when loss occurs. It's where you will find comfort from those who truly understand the grief of losing a "fallen hero" as well as respect for the life and the service of our loved ones, who had the character, courage, and ability to selflessly serve in the cause of freedom.

Because grief doesn't keep regular hours, TAPS is available 24/7 through the National Military Survivor Helpline at 800-959-TAPS (8277). We understand that sometimes it's more difficult in the middle of the night or on special days like Mother's Day or Father's Day, or during the holidays, when there is an empty seat at the family table. When you reach out to TAPS, someone at the other end of the line will listen, understand, and help.

TAPS connects survivors through national networks of comfort and care, both in person and by phone, email, online chats, social media groups, and texting. Our award-winning quarterly magazine, available at no cost to survivors, shares news and articles by both professionals and survivors. We also get together in person throughout the year at Regional Survivor Seminars that explore the grief journey and offer guidance on coping strategies. Retreats bring us together based on our relationship to the person who died (parents, siblings, spouses and significant others, and adult children) in beautiful outdoor settings to find hope and healing in nature. And Good Grief Camps and Camp Outs give surviving children, youth, and teens the coping skills and friendships they need to heal.

Since military deaths can also create practical challenges such as financial hardships and career changes, TAPS can connect you with emergency assistance, pro bono legal support, spouse and child education benefits, guidance in applying for additional aid, employment assistance, and much more. TAPS joins forces with military casualty offices and the Department of Veterans Affairs to expedite issues to quick resolution.

TAPS can also provide you with a soft landing in your hometown by carefully researching and connecting you with all the grief support programs available wherever you may live, no matter how small or remote your town may be. TAPS is also able to arrange additional support with a local professional grief counselor who will provide services for you at no cost.

TAPS is our family, for all of us who are honoring our loved one's life and service as we grieve their passing. We are here for each other, now and always. What we remember most is the love, what we celebrate is the life, and what we do now is share the journey together, as a family.

How to use this book

We wrote this book to help you embrace your grief in positive, proactive ways and to companion you on the journey to reconciling your loss and healing. It contains 100 practical thoughts and ideas to help you understand your unique grief in the aftermath of a military death and, even more important, to express it. Grief expressed is called *mourning*, and mourning helps you heal. Grief repressed or kept inside, on the other hand, leads to chronic emotional, spiritual, and physical problems.

We invite you to flip this book open to any page. Read through the Idea you encounter and determine if it speaks to your unique grief journey. If it doesn't, try another Idea. If it does, try the exercise described in the *carpe diem* (which is Latin for "seize the day"). The carpe diem exercises are there to help you do something with your grief, right here and now, empowering you to be an active participant in your own healing.

And if you are able to muster the courage to actively mourn, you will heal. And you will grow. And you will love and live again. Remember, you are not alone. Many others have not only survived the death of a loved one, but have also chosen to truly live. Find ways to reach out to these people. Find ways to share your experience. Find ways to make connections.

God bless you. We hope to meet you one day.

Bonnie Carroll

Alan D. Wolfelt

BONNIE'S STORY

A LIFE SHATTERED. A LIVING LEGACY BORN.

In November 1992, the world I knew—a joyous life with an extraordinary husband—suddenly ceased to be. Tom, the commanding general of the Alaska Army National Guard, and seven other soldiers were traveling on a routine mission when their aircraft crashed into the side of a mountain, killing all on board. The shock of their deaths was more than I felt I could bear.

Tom was larger than life, compassionate and kind, and incredibly strong both physically and mentally. Soldiers such as Tom should surely be immortal; they should grow old and become elder statesmen, and then die peacefully, surrounded by those they love. It should not end like this. It could not end like this. It was impossible for me to conceive that he was gone, much less reconcile that this was now my life, without him.

Thousands attended the memorial service. Our grief was public, something to be watched on television and seen on the front page of the newspaper. Strangers offered heartfelt condolences. But through it all, I felt that surely this wasn't happening to us. It could not be real.

As the weeks went on, new soldiers were promoted to fill the vacant positions, and everyone seemed to be focused on "moving on." But all I wanted so desperately was for time not just to stand still, but to go backward. Back to "before," when all was right with the world—when, as I fantasized, I could have done something to change what was about to happen. Grief does that. It turns the world upside down and inside out, and nothing feels quite right at all.

Because there were eight families profoundly impacted in that single tragedy, we had the gift of an immediate peer support network. We found that in our little group, there was no judgment, no small talk, no triviality. We had looked death in the face, and it was devastating. We had lost everything. We had big things to figure out, and we were grateful to have each other. Grief strips us down to our bare souls. It removes all the things that really don't matter. And it connects us as though we are now speaking some secret language that only those with a grieving heart can understand.

And so we remembered together, we cried together, we laughed together, and we made memorials to the men we love. That is the power of peer support. It is the gift of freedom to grieve as we must, with love and honesty and the support of those who speak this newfound language of loss.

In 1992, there was no place for those who have lost a loved one in the military to go to find the safety we felt in our little group. I attended gatherings of the Concerns of Police Survivors (COPS), and while they were grieving their heroes who died in public service, it just wasn't the same. I tried attending hospice groups, cancer loss groups, even a group for victims of homicide. Nothing resonated. That wasn't my experience. They weren't speaking my language. I joined Gold Star Wives and the Society of Military Widows, membership organizations focused on the important work of ensuring benefits for widows, not the immediate work of grieving a traumatic death.

And so the journey began, to create an organization that would focus on those areas the other groups weren't addressing, not to replicate their good works but to collaborate with them. A new organization would fill the gaps in service provided by federal, state, and private sources, with their guidance and support. The Tragedy Assistance Program for Survivors, or TAPS, was formally launched on the two-year anniversary of the Alaska Army National Guard's worst loss, with a charter to provide hope and healing to all who are grieving a death in the Armed Forces.

TAPS's mission is to warmly welcome those with a grieving heart, who speak the secret language of military loss, into a family where there is no judgment. One can call at two o'clock in the morning and reach a peer ready to listen, find support in their local communities, or connect to a national network of other survivors. TAPS offers casework assistance to navigate challenging bureaucracies and opportunities to attend survivor seminars, camps, and retreats around the country.

My Tom was a bold leader. He was a visionary. He was also a kind soldier who cared for his troops. Each of our men and women in uniform has done something extraordinary with their lives. They have stepped out above the rest of society in character, courage, honor, and ability to serve in the cause of freedom. Regardless of how or where they died, they were on duty for this great nation at the moment of their death.

And now, the hard part is on us. We must grieve and mourn their deaths, honor their service, and forever remember and cherish the gift it was to have their love in our life. We are their living legacy.

1.

UNDERSTAND WHAT IT MEANS TO BE "TRAUMATIZED"

"There are wounds that never show on the body that are deeper and more hurtful than anything that bleeds."
— Laurell K. Hamilton

• You've been traumatized by a sudden and likely violent death. We are so sorry for your loss.

• How is your grief this time different from your past experience with anticipated or non-violent deaths? As you know, the death of someone loved always causes painful feelings. But in the case of sudden, violent death, your mind has an especially difficult time acknowledging and absorbing the circumstances of the death itself. This is especially true of military deaths because they often happen far away, in places and circumstances that aren't completely knowable or understandable.

• In this sense, the word "trauma" refers to intense feelings of shock, fear, anxiety, and helplessness surrounding the cause of death. Trauma is caused by events of such intensity or magnitude of horror that they would overwhelm any human being's capacity to cope.

• Certainly it can be said that death is always traumatic. Even the natural death of an aged parent can feel traumatic to her children. But sudden and violent deaths result in a kind of psychic injury. They often cause frightening, intrusive thoughts about the distressful event that caused the death. (For more on traumatic grief, please see Idea 3.)

CARPE DIEM

If you have been having frightening or intrusive thoughts about the death, share them with someone else today. Be gentle with yourself as you work to acknowledge the reality of the nature of the death.

11

2.

FIRST, SEEK SAFETY AND COMFORT

"After a traumatic experience, the human system of self-preservation seems to go onto permanent alert, as if the danger might return at any moment."
— Judith Lewis Herman

- After a traumatic experience, it's natural to feel vulnerable, unsafe, and anxious. Your nervous system is telling your brain and body that the world isn't a safe place right now. Your fight-or-flight response has been activated, sending fear and anxiety biochemicals cascading through your body. Yet there is nothing for you to fight or flee from.

- To overcome your trauma, you must locate yourself among people and in places that make you feel safe. If this means moving in with a friend or relative temporarily, that's OK. If this means avoiding certain places or people for now, that's OK, too.

- What calms and comforts you? Taking a walk? Hugging your pet? Relaxing in the tub? Yoga or meditation or prayer? Identify activities that soothe you and turn to them when your anxiety is high.

- You will not be able to mourn and move toward healing if you feel unsafe or overly anxious. Seek safety and comfort first, then you can begin to slowly embrace your grief. If you are having ongoing struggles with anxiety and other fear-based symptoms, especially if those symptoms are preventing you from functioning in your daily life, please seek the assistance of a professional counselor right away. There is help and there is hope.

CARPE DIEM
Let someone else take care of you today.
It's normal and natural to need help with the activities of daily living in the early days and weeks after a traumatic death.

3.

BE AWARE OF POST-TRAUMATIC STRESS

"PTSD is all about being stuck in the moment of horror, unable to move past it. The feeling is very much like being trapped in a nightmare, unable to wake up, or like a computer that's frozen and incapable of functioning."
— Unknown

- Sudden, violent deaths can cause extreme grief reactions in survivors. Not only people who serve in the military but also their families at home may end up suffering from what is commonly called PSTD.

- Post-traumatic stress disorder, or PTSD, is a term used to describe the psychological condition that survivors of sudden, violent death sometimes experience. People with PTSD often have nightmares or scary thoughts about the terrible experience they or their loved one went through. They try to stay away from anything that reminds them of the frightening experience. They often feel angry and are unable to care about or trust other people. They may be on the lookout for danger and get very upset when something happens without warning. Their anxiety level is continually high.

- The more you learn about trauma and PTSD, the more you will have some sense of control at a time when you naturally feel out of control. Knowledge is one of the best antidotes to anxiety, fear, and depression.

- I (Alan) prefer the term "traumatic grief" to PTSD because I do not think that it is a disorder. Instead, it is a normal and necessary response to an abnormally brutal reality.

- If you think you may have PTSD, talk to your family doctor or a counselor. You may need therapy and/or medication for a time to help you feel safer and cope with your day-to-day life. You will need to get help for your PTSD before you can deal with grief and mourning.

CARPE DIEM

If you think you or someone in your family might be suffering from traumatic grief or PTSD, we suggest you call TAPS at 800-959-8277. They can connect you to a counselor who has experience helping military family members with traumatic grief.

4.

UNDERSTAND THE DIFFERENCE BETWEEN GRIEF AND MOURNING

"Grief is like the ocean. It comes in waves, ebbing and flowing. Sometimes the water is calm, and sometimes it is overwhelming. All we can do is learn to swim."

— Vicki Harrison

- Grief is what we think and feel inside when someone loved dies. Grief lives inside us.

- Mourning is the outward expression of our grief. Mourning is crying, talking about the death, journaling, participating in a support group, and other forms of expression. Mourning is the grief we allow to venture outside us. Mourning is grief in motion.

- Everyone grieves when someone loved dies, but if we are to heal, we must also mourn.

- Many of the ideas in this book are intended to help you mourn this death, to express your feelings of trauma and grief outside of yourself. Over time and with the support of others, to mourn is to heal.

- Mourn the death while remaining sensitive to your unique needs as a trauma survivor. You will need to be very compassionate and patient with yourself in the months and years to come. Give yourself the gift of time. While time alone doesn't heal wounds, healing does take time.

CARPE DIEM
Ask yourself this: Have I been mourning this death or have I restricted myself to grieving?

5.

BE AWARE THAT YOUR GRIEF AFFECTS YOUR BODY, MIND, HEART, SOCIAL SELF, AND SPIRIT

"She has been surprised by grief, its constancy, its immediacy, its unrelenting physical pain."
— Michelle Latiolais

- Grief is physically demanding. This is especially true with traumatic grief. Your body responds to the stress of the encounter, and the immune system can weaken. You may be more susceptible to illness and physical discomforts. You may also feel lethargic, weak, or extremely fatigued. You may not be sleeping well and you may have little appetite (or you may be overeating). Your stomach may hurt. Your chest may ache.

- Cognitively, you may have trouble thinking clearly. Your thoughts may seem disorganized, and you might be finding it hard to concentrate or complete even the simplest task.

- Likewise, the emotional toll of grief is complex and painful. You may feel many different feelings, and those feelings can shift and blur over time.

- This death has probably also caused social discomfort. Because they don't know what to say or do, some friends and family members may withdraw from you, leaving you isolated and unsupported.

- You may ask yourself, "Why go on living?" "Will my life have meaning now?" "Where is God in this?" Spiritual questions such as these are natural and necessary but also draining.

- Basically, your grief will affect every aspect of your life. Don't be alarmed. Trust that if you do your grief work and meet your needs of mourning, you will find peace and comfort again.

CARPE DIEM

If you've felt physically affected by your grief, see a doctor this week. Sometimes it's comforting to receive a clean bill of health. Or, if you need some physical care, get it. Remember, your body is sometimes smarter than your head; it will let you know when you need rest and care.

6.

UNDERSTAND THAT GRIEF FOLLOWING A TRAUMATIC DEATH IS PARTICULARLY DIFFICULT

"Here is one of the worst things about having someone you love die.
It happens again every single morning."
— Anna Quindlen

• Not only has someone you love died, but the death may have been sudden and violent. The traumatic aspects of the death will likely make your grief journey especially painful.

• As we've said, grief is the collection of thoughts and feelings you have on the inside after someone dies. This includes the thoughts and feelings you have about the circumstances of the death itself. This aspect of your grief may consume most of your energies, especially in the early weeks and months following the death.

• Even much later, after you've come to terms with the nature of the death, it will always be a significant part of your grief.

• Remember that just as your feelings of grief need to be expressed, so do your feelings of trauma. Your trauma is part of your grief and also needs to be mourned.

CARPE DIEM
If today, or at any point in your grief journey, you feel like this death and your grief are so hurtful and horrific that you can't cope, take this as a sign that you need to reach out for help. Call a friend or a spiritual mentor, participate in an online support group, or see an experienced grief counselor right away. TAPS staffs a 24-hour helpline.
Call anytime if you need help of any kind: 800-959-8277.

7.

ALLOW FOR NUMBNESS

"Only when someone very near and dear to one leaves does one appreciate the stark tragedy of death. Even then, nature tends to cushion the initial shock, and the thought 'he is gone' does not carry the later realization of finality and permanence that comes only with the final, indisputable understanding that 'we will never see him again.'"

—General Jimmy Doolittle

- Feelings of shock, numbness, and disbelief are nature's way of temporarily protecting us from the full reality of a sudden, violent death. They help us survive our early grief.

- We often think, "I will wake up and this will not have happened." Early grief can feel like being in a dream.

- Your emotions need time to catch up with what your mind has been told.

- Even after you have moved beyond these initial feelings, don't be surprised if they reemerge. Birthdays, holidays, and anniversaries often trigger these normal and necessary feelings.

- Trauma loss often goes beyond what we consider "normal" shock. In fact, you may experience what is called psychic numbing—the deadening or shutting off of emotions. Your sense that "this isn't happening to me" may persist for months, sometimes even years. Don't set rigid expectations for yourself and your ability to function "normally" in the world around you.

- Think of shock and numbness as a bandage that your psyche has placed over your wound. The bandage protects the wound until it has become less open and raw. Only after healing has begun and a scab has formed can the bandage be removed and the wound openly exposed to the world.

CARPE DIEM

If you're feeling numb, cancel any commitments that require concentration and decision-making. Allow yourself time to regroup.

8.

CONSIDER YOURSELF IN "EMOTIONAL INTENSIVE CARE"

"And the bad news is that you never completely get over the loss of your beloved. But this is also the good news. They live forever in your broken heart that doesn't seal back up. And you come through. It's like having a broken leg that never heals perfectly—that still hurts when the weather gets cold—but you learn to dance with the limp."

— Anne Lamott

- Something catastrophic has happened in your life. Something assaulting to the very core of your being. Something excruciatingly painful.

- Your spirit has been deeply injured. Just as your body could not be expected to recover immediately after a brutal injury, neither can your psyche.

- Imagine that you've suffered a severe physical injury and are in your hospital's intensive care unit. Your friends and family surround you with their presence and love. The medical staff attends to you constantly. Your body rests and recovers.

- This is the kind of care you need and deserve right now. The blow you have suffered is no less devastating than this imagined physical injury. Allow others to take care of you. Ask for their help. Give yourself as much resting time as possible. Take time off work if at all possible. Let household chores slide. In the early weeks and months after the death, don't expect—indeed, don't try—to carry on with your normal routine.

CARPE DIEM

Close your eyes and imagine yourself in "emotional intensive care."
Where are you? What kind of care are you receiving? From whom?
Try to arrange a weekend or a week of the emotional
and spiritual intensive care you most need.

9.

UNDERSTAND THE SIX NEEDS OF MOURNING

Need 1: Acknowledge the reality of the death

"Believe in the wonderment of life, the magic of love,
and the reality of death."
— Carroll Bryant

- Your first need of mourning is to gently confront the difficult reality that someone you love is dead and will never physically be present to you again.

- Even when a death is anticipated, acknowledging the full reality of the loss may take weeks or months. Accepting the reality of sudden and violent deaths usually takes longer.

- You will first come to acknowledge the reality of the loss with your head. Only over time will you come to acknowledge it with your heart. As Stephen Levine has noted, "There are pains that cannot be contained in the mind, only in the heart."

- At times you may push away the reality of the death. This is normal. You will come to integrate the reality in doses as you are ready.

- You may be saying to yourself, "I feel like I'm dreaming. I keep hoping I'll wake up and none of this will have happened." We hear this often from trauma survivors. Your shock protects you from being overwhelmed by the loss. You need and deserve time to reconstitute yourself after this traumatic death. You need time to become accustomed to thinking and feeling in your new reality. Go slow. There are no rewards for speed.

CARPE DIEM
Tell someone about the death today. Talking about it will
help you work on this important need.

19

10.

UNDERSTAND THE SIX NEEDS
OF MOURNING

Need 2: Embrace the pain of the loss

"The cure for pain is in the pain."
— Rumi

- This need of mourning requires us to embrace the pain of our loss— something we naturally don't want to do. It is easier to avoid, repress, or push away the pain of grief than it is to confront it.

- It is in embracing your grief, however, that you will learn to reconcile yourself to it.

- You will need to slowly—ever so slowly—"dose" yourself in embracing your pain. If you were to allow in all the pain at once, you could not survive.

- People with chronic physical pain are taught not to tighten around the pain but to relax and allow the pain to be present. When pain is resist-ed, it intensifies. You don't want to fight with your pain; you want to allow it into your soul in small doses so that eventually you can move from darkness into light.

CARPE DIEM
If you feel up to it, allow yourself some time for embracing pain today. Dedicate 15 minutes to doing nothing but thinking about and feeling the loss. Reach out to someone who doesn't try to take your pain away and share your thoughts and feelings with him.

11.

UNDERSTAND THE SIX NEEDS OF MOURNING

Need 3: Remember the person who died

"Your silent tents of green
We deck with fragrant flowers;
Yours has the suffering been,
The memory shall be ours."
— Henry Wadsworth Longfellow

- When someone loved dies, they live on in us through memory.

- To heal, you need to actively remember the person who died and commemorate the life that was lived.

- Never let anyone take your memories away in a misguided attempt to save you from pain. It's good for you to continue to display photos of the person who died. It's good to talk about him. It's good to save belongings and mementos of his life.

- Remembering the past makes hoping for the future possible. As Danish philosopher and theologian Søren Kierkegaard noted, "Life can only be understood backwards, but it must be lived forwards."

CARPE DIEM
Brainstorm a list of characteristics or memories of the
person who died. Write as fast as you can for 10 minutes (or more),
then put away your list for later reflection.

12.

UNDERSTAND THE SIX NEEDS
OF MOURNING

Need 4: Develop a new self-identity

*"She stood in the storm, and when the wind did not blow her away—
and it surely has not—she adjusted her sails."*
— Elizabeth Edwards

• Part of your self-identity was formed by the relationship you had with the person who died.

• You may have gone from being a "wife" to a "widow" or from a "parent" to a "bereaved parent." The way you thought of yourself and the way society thinks of you has changed.

• The part of your identity that was shaped by your military status or affiliation is also morphing. The military is very good at creating a strong culture—regulations and processes and ways of talking and thinking that bind military members and their families together. This culture may have given you a sense of belonging. But now that your military ties may be dissolving, what does that mean for the part of you that identified as a military family member?

• You need to re-anchor yourself, to reconstruct your self-identity. This is arduous and painful work. One of your biggest challenges may be to recreate yourself in the face of the loss of who you once were. Let us assure you that you can and will do this.

• Many mourners discover that as they work on this need, they ultimately discover some positive changes to their self-identities, such as becoming more caring or less judgmental.

CARPE DIEM
Write out a response to this prompt: I used to be _____.
Now that _____ died, I am _____. This makes me feel
_____. Keep writing as long as you want.

13.

UNDERSTAND THE SIX NEEDS OF MOURNING

Need 5: Search for meaning

"Why? Parents all over the earth who lost sons in the war have felt this kind of question, and sought an answer. To me, it means loving life more, being more aware of life, of one's fellow human beings, of the earth."

— Frances Gunther

- When someone loved dies, we naturally question the meaning and purpose of life and death. It's hard—maybe even impossible—to make sense of a death that can seem so senseless. While some people find profound meaning in the idea of sacrifice to country, others struggle with what can seem like the squandering of a precious life. And it's not uncommon for survivors to feel a little of both! Regardless of your feelings about the circumstances of the death, it is normal and necessary to struggle with the "why" and try to find meaning.

- "Why?" questions often precede "How" questions. "Why did this happen?" comes before "How will I go on living?"

- You will probably question your philosophy of life and explore religious and spiritual values as you work on this need. You may also find yourself questioning the military's rationale or decision-making that contributed to your loved one's death. After someone you love is taken from you, it's normal to question.

- Remember that having faith or spirituality does not negate your need to mourn. "Blessed are those who mourn for they shall be comforted."

- Some people may tell you that asking "Why?" doesn't do you any good. These people are usually unfamiliar with the experience of traumatic grief. Try to reach out to people who can create a supportive atmosphere for you right now.

CARPE DIEM
Write down a list of "why" questions that have surfaced for you since the death. Find a friend or counselor who will explore these questions with you without thinking she has to give you answers.

14.

UNDERSTAND THE SIX NEEDS OF MOURNING

Need 6: Receive ongoing support from others

"Gracious acceptance is an art—an art which most never bother to cultivate. We think that we have to learn how to give, but we forget about accepting things, which can be much harder than giving... Accepting another person's gift is allowing him to express his feelings for you."
— Alexander McCall Smith

- As mourners, we need the love and understanding of others if we are to heal.
- Don't feel ashamed by your dependence on others right now. Instead, revel in the knowledge that others care about you.
- Unfortunately, our society places too much value on "carrying on" and "doing well" after a death. Because of this, many mourners are abandoned by their friends and family soon after the death. It has been said that grief rewrites your address book.
- One of the touchstones of grief is that each and every one of us as humans are connected by loss. As you experience the physical separation from someone you love, you are connected to every single person who has experienced or ever will experience a similar loss. Part of the TAPS motto encourages us to "share the journey."
- When others offer to help, tell them something practical they can do, such as babysit, grocery shop, or mow the lawn.
- Grief is a process, not an event, and you will need the continued support of your friends and family for weeks, months, and years.

CARPE DIEM
Sometimes your friends and family want to support you but don't know *how*. Ask. Call your closest friend right now and tell him you need his help through the coming weeks and months.

15.

KNOW THAT GRIEF DOES NOT PROCEED IN ORDERLY, PREDICTABLE "STAGES"

"Grief is not tidy steps; it's not evenly spaced or surefooted stages or rooms we walk through... It's taking one step forward and falling three steps back. It's falling down and getting back up again. It's determining to live one moment at a time... It takes a lot of energy. It takes a lot of time."

— Rebecca R. Carney

- Though the "Needs of Mourning" (Ideas 9-14) are numbered 1-6, grief is not an orderly progression towards healing. Don't fall into the trap of thinking your grief journey will be predictable or always forward-moving.

- You may have heard of the "stages" of grief, popularized in 1969 by Elisabeth Kübler-Ross's landmark text, *On Death and Dying*. In this book she lists the five stages of grief that she saw terminally ill patients experience in the face of their own impending deaths: denial, anger, bargaining, depression, and acceptance. However, she never intended for her five stages to be applied to all grief or to be interpreted as a rigid, linear sequence to be followed by all mourners.

- Usually, grief hurts more before it hurts less. This is because the initial numbing eventually wears off, often right about the time when friends and family withdraw their support, assuming you are doing better.

- You will probably experience a multitude of different emotions in a wave-like fashion. You will also likely encounter more than one need of mourning at the same time. Understandably, survivors of sudden, violent death also tend to spend more time and effort on the first need of mourning: acknowledging the reality of the death.

- Be compassionate with yourself as you experience your own unique grief journey.

CARPE DIEM
Has anyone told you that you are in this or that "stage" of grief? Ignore this usually well-intended advice. Don't allow yourself or anyone else to compartmentalize your grief.

16.

DON'T EXPECT YOURSELF TO MOURN OR HEAL IN A CERTAIN WAY OR IN A CERTAIN TIME

"No rule book. No time frame. Grief is as individual as a fingerprint.
Do what is right for your soul."
— Unknown

- Your unique grief journey will be shaped by many factors, including:
  - the nature of the relationship you had with the person who died.
  - the age of the person who died.
  - the specific circumstances of the death.
  - your unique personality.
  - your cultural background.
  - your religious or spiritual beliefs.
  - your gender.
  - your support systems.

- Because of these and other factors, no two deaths are ever grieved and mourned in precisely the same way. Even two military deaths can result in quite different experiences for those left behind.

- Don't have rigid expectations for your thoughts, feelings, and behaviors. Don't have rigid expectations for the thoughts, feelings, and behaviors of others, either. If you have friends or family members who aren't mourning in the ways you think they should be, try to keep in mind that there is no one right way to grieve and mourn. Everyone's journey through grief is different.

CARPE DIEM
Talk to someone else mourning this death—perhaps
someone whose mourning style is very different from your own.
Compare notes about your grief journeys.

17.

TAKE GOOD CARE OF YOURSELF

*"Self love is asking yourself what you need—every day—
and then making sure you receive it."*
— Unknown

- Good self-care is nurturing and necessary for mourners, yet it's something many of us completely overlook.

- Try very hard to eat well and get adequate rest. Lay your body down two to three times a day for 20 to 30 minutes, even if you don't sleep. We know—you probably don't care very much about eating well right now, and you may be sleeping poorly. But taking care of yourself is truly one way to fuel healing and begin to embrace life again.

- Listen to what your body tells you. "Get some rest," it says. "But I don't have time," you reply. "I have things to do." "OK, then, I'll get sick so you HAVE to rest," your body says. And it *will* get sick if that's what it takes to get its needs met.

- Drink at least five to six glasses of water each day. Dehydration can compound feelings of fatigue and disorientation.

- Exercise not only provides you with more energy, it can give you focused thinking time. Take a 20-minute walk every day. Or, if that seems too much, a five-minute walk. But don't over-exercise, because your body needs extra rest as well.

- Now more than ever, you need to allow time for you.

CARPE DIEM
Are you taking a multivitamin?
If not, now is probably a good time to start.

18.

IF YOU SAW THE BODY AND ITS INJURIES, GIVE YOURSELF TIME TO CONJURE UP HAPPIER MEMORIES

"Grief can destroy you—or focus you. You can decide a relationship was all for nothing if it had to end in death…Or you can realize that every moment of it had more meaning that you dared to recognize at the time."

— Dean Koontz

- After a sudden, violent death, family members who viewed the body are often glad they did. The military mortuary in Dover, Delaware, is highly experienced at preparing bodies for viewing. Many times the injuries are not as disfiguring as the family had imagined. And being able to hold and kiss and touch the body one last time helped them acknowledge the reality of the death.

- Other people choose not to see the body. Trust that if you were given the choice, you made the choice that was right for you.

- Still, you may find yourself unable to shake the image of the person's dead body. You may find yourself returning to this photographic memory over and over again. This is normal. In time you will spontaneously recall happier images of the person you loved. If you don't, you may find it helpful to seek the assistance of a compassionate counselor.

- A note for fellow service members or families touched by suicide: If you actually witnessed the injuries and the death as they were occurring, or if you were the person to find the body, you have special needs that may best be addressed with an experienced trauma or grief counselor. This is not in any way to imply that something is wrong with you, but rather that your experience was so extreme that you may need additional support.

CARPE DIEM
Spend some time looking at photos of the person who died. Set aside an hour or two to linger over albums today. Or better yet, watch family videos that include the person who died.

19.

IF YOU WEREN'T ABLE TO SEE THE BODY, FIND OTHER WAYS TO ACKNOWLEDGE THE REALITY OF THE DEATH

"No person was ever honored for what he received.
Honor has been the reward for what he gave."
— Calvin Coolidge

• In some cases of military death, family members are unable to view the body. Perhaps the body could not be recovered at all. Or maybe it was so damaged that medical and military staff convinced you not to view it.

• One problem with never seeing the body is that you may struggle with feelings that the person isn't really dead. After all, the last time you saw him he was alive and healthy. How could he be dead? Maybe the person who was buried or cremated wasn't really him, you may think (despite all objective evidence to the contrary), and he'll show up on your doorstep one day soon.

• Another problem with never viewing the body is that your mind is forced to imagine what the body looked like. Your imagination may be worse than reality.

• I (Alan) often say that our minds can cope with what they know, but they cannot cope with what they could not see or what has been kept from them. If you weren't able to view the body, maybe it would help you to read the coroner's report or to have someone read it for you and tell you in layman's terms what the injuries were like. If photos are available and you feel ready, you may want to view them with a trusted friend, grief counselor, or physician. Or perhaps you could talk to the doctors, nurses, or service members who recovered and cared for the body.

CARPE DIEM
If you have lingering, unexpressed thoughts and feelings about
never having seen the body, talk about them with someone you trust.
Sometimes simply giving voice to your concerns renders them less
powerful. This person may also be able to help you learn more
about the condition of the body.

20.

USE LANGUAGE THAT EMPOWERS YOU

"Words and hearts should be handled with care, for words when spoken and hearts when broken are the hardest things to repair."
— Unknown

- Sometimes the language we choose affects how we think and feel about our lives. Passive language can make us feel even more victimized. Stronger language can help us regain some sense of control.

- After a military death, we may find some military lingo or euphemisms hurtful. Terms like "collateral damage," "casualty," "engagement," "friendly fire," "fallen warrior," "committed suicide," and even "ultimate sacrifice" can sometimes seem, when they are applied to the very real death of the unique and precious person we love, more like disingenuousness.

- When you think or speak about the death, choose words that feel right to you and empower you. In general, we have found that euphemisms such as "passed away" are less helpful to our healing than words that acknowledge the reality, like "died" and "killed."

- Similarly, work to find words to describe how you're really feeling. When someone asks "How are you?", learn to be brief but honest. Say, "I've been feeling really (sad, angry, lonely, etc.)." Or "This week was hard for me because…" Saying "I'm fine" or "I'm doing OK" may not serve you or the listener well.

CARPE DIEM

Are there certain words that people use when talking about the death that bother you? The next time you hear them, let the speaker know why this terminology is painful to you.

21.

IGNORE HURTFUL COMMENTS

"It has been said 'time heals all wounds.' I do not agree. The wounds remain. In time, the mind, protecting its sanity, covers them with scar tissue, and the pain lessens, but it is never gone."

— Rose Kennedy

- Sometimes well-intentioned but misinformed family, friends, and community members will hurt you unknowingly with their words:
    - I know just how you feel.
    - He would want you to get on with your life.
    - Keep your chin up.
    - It was God's will.
    - It was her time to go.
    - God always takes the good ones first.
    - Be glad it was quick.
    - Think of all you have to be thankful for.
    - Now you have an angel in heaven.
    - Time heals all wounds.
    - God wouldn't give you more than you can handle.
    - You're strong. You'll get through this.
    - You're young. You can get married again.
- After a military death, even the common, respectful response "Thank you for your loved one's service" or "Thank you for your sacrifice" can seem hurtfully vague, generic, or trite. And because the military is inextricably tied to foreign policy, you may even hear comments like, "It was such a waste" or "What did you expect? He enlisted!"
- When comments are hurtful or dismissive, don't take them to heart. They are usually offered because people don't know any better or don't know what else to say. The problem is, phrases like these diminish the significance of your grief.

CARPE DIEM

The next time someone unknowingly hurts you with their words,
try responding with kind honesty. For example, if someone
tells you "Time heals all wounds," you might say,
"I will miss _____ every day for the rest of my life."

22.

REACH OUT AND TOUCH

*"I've learned that every day you should reach out and touch someone.
People love a warm hug or just a friendly pat on the back."*
— Maya Angelou

- For many people, physical contact with another human being is healing. It has been recognized since ancient times as having transformative, healing powers.

- Have you hugged anyone lately? Held someone's hand? Put your arm around another human being?

- You probably know several people who enjoy hugging or physical touching. If you're comfortable with their touch, encourage it in the weeks and months to come.

- Hug someone you feel safe with. Kiss your children or a friend's baby. Walk arm in arm with a neighbor.

- You may want to listen to the song titled "I Know What Love Is," by Don White. I (Alan) have found this song helps me reflect on the power of touch. Listen to this song then drop me a note or e-mail (drwolfelt@centerforloss.com) and let me know how it makes you think and, more important, feel.

CARPE DIEM
Try hugging your close friends and family members today, even if you usually don't. Notice how it makes you feel.

23.

KEEP A JOURNAL

"When your heart speaks, take good notes."
— Joseph Campbell

- Journals are an ideal way for some mourners to record thoughts and feelings.

- Remember—your inner thoughts and feelings of grief need to be expressed outwardly (which can include writing) if you are to heal.

- Consider jotting down your thoughts and feelings first thing when you wake up or each night before you go to sleep. Your journal entries can be as long or as short as you want.

- Don't worry about what you're writing or how well you're writing it. Just write whatever comes into your mind. To get started, set a timer for five or ten minutes and write as much as you can without stopping.

- Sometimes it can feel like you're stuck in your grief. Keeping a journal allows you to look back at entries from last month or last year and see the progress you're making.

CARPE DIEM

Stop by your local book or stationery store and choose a blank book you like the look and feel of. Visit a park on your way home, find a quiet bench, and write your first entry.

24.

LET GO OF DESTRUCTIVE MISCONCEPTIONS ABOUT GRIEF AND MOURNING

"Grief is not a disorder, a disease, or a sign of weakness. It is an emotional, physical, and spiritual necessity, the price you pay for love."
— Earl Grollman

- Most of us have internalized a number of our society's harmful misconceptions about grief and mourning.

- Here are some to let go of:
  - I need to be strong and carry on.
  - Tears are a sign of weakness.
  - I need to get over my grief.
  - Death is something we don't talk about.
  - The more traumatic the death, the more I should try to put it behind me quickly and efficiently.
  - Other people need me so I need to "hurry up" and get back to my "normal" self.

- Sometimes these misconceptions will cause you to feel guilty about or ashamed of your true thoughts and feelings.

- Your grief is your grief. It's normal and necessary. Allow it to be what it is.

CARPE DIEM
Which grief misconception has been most harmful to your grief journey so far? Consider the ways in which you could help teach others about these destructive misconceptions.

25.

IF YOU ARE A FELLOW SERVICE MEMBER, GET EXTRA SUPPORT

"Greater love has no one than this: to lay down one's life for one's friends."
— The Gospel According to John, 15:13

- If you were a battle buddy of a military service member who was killed, most of the guidance about grief in this book applies to you. But you may also have additional mourning needs.

- In a million different ways, service members have a tough job, but nothing is tougher than having someone you care about and feel responsible for die while serving.

- If you have witnessed violence and death firsthand, you need and deserve support in working through the trauma of these experiences. No human being, even trained combat personnel, can live through such horror without suffering psychological and spiritual injuries. You may well be on grief overload (see Idea 58).

- Even if you were not there when the death occurred, as a military insider you have special needs. You are likely to feel guilt and maybe anger. You are subject to a military culture that might encourage you to hide or deny your grief.

CARPE DIEM

If you had suffered a serious physical injury, you would go to the doctor or hospital, right? You have suffered a serious emotional and spiritual injury. You need and deserve excellent emotional and spiritual care, so we encourage you to see an experienced grief counselor. Vet Centers across America offer confidential counseling at no cost to you.

26.

EMBRACE YOUR NEED AND RIGHT TO GRIEVE AND MOURN

"So it's true, when all is said and done, grief is the price we pay for love."
— E. A. Bucchianeri

• Whenever you lose something you value and are attached to, you grieve. That makes grief love's conjoined twin.

• You can't love without one day grieving. To welcome love into your life means that you also have to welcome grief. They're two sides of the same precious coin.

• Think of it this way: If love is a privilege, then so is grief.

• You embraced your need and right to love. Now it's time to embrace your need and right to grieve and mourn.

CARPE DIEM
Right now, close your eyes and allow your grief thoughts and feelings—whatever they are today—to wash over you. Welcome them. Then go tell someone how you feel.

27.

BELIEVE IN THE POWER OF STORY

"Sometimes reality is too complex. Stories give it form."
— Jean Luc Godard

- A vital part of healing in grief is often "telling the story" over and over again. For military death survivors, the shock of the death may delay your need to talk about it for months, even years.

- In cases of sudden and violent death, you may feel compelled to think and talk about the circumstances of the death itself. This is normal and necessary. Your mind returns to the moment of the death in an effort to fathom that which is unfathomable.

- What if you don't want to talk about it? It's OK to respect this feeling for a while, but eventually you'll need to start talking about it. Keeping your thoughts and feelings about the death inside you only makes them more powerful. Trust that you will "tell your story" when you are ready.

- Over time, your grief story will likely evolve from one dominated by the death itself to one dominated by loving memories of the person who died. This is a natural progression and a sign that you are healing.

- Find people who are willing to listen to you tell your story, over and over again if necessary, without judgment. These are often "fellow strugglers" who have had similar losses. But remember that not everyone will be able to be a compassionate listener. Seek out listeners who can be present to your pain.

CARPE DIEM
Today, discuss the story of the death with someone else who
loved the person who died. This person may also be struggling
with painful questions and fears regarding the circumstances
of the death. Listen to and support each other.

28.

IF THIS DEATH HAS PUT YOUR FAMILY IN THE MEDIA SPOTLIGHT, APPOINT SOMEONE TO HANDLE MEDIA INQUIRIES

"There are some who've forgotten why we have a military.
It's not to promote war. It's to be prepared for peace."
— President Ronald Reagan

- Often military deaths are front-page news. Over and over you may hear about the death on TV, on the car radio, or in your newspaper. This phenomenon tends to make families feel as if they have no privacy, and the coverage can re-traumatize you.

- The public realm may have laid claim to this death, but it is still first and foremost your personal loss. Focus on your family's grief. Focus on your own physical, cognitive, emotional, social, and spiritual well-being. Do what feels right for you.

- New survivors, particularly survivors of suicide loss, are often asked to comment on the "why" of the death. Because of this, you might want to consider refraining from speaking to the media until you are further along in the grieving process.

- Some families find that in being open with the media, they are able to share their personal stories in a way that helps both them and the community mourn. Other families find that to mourn and heal, they must withdraw and grieve more privately among close family and friends. We trust that you will do what is right for you and your family.

- Be assertive with media representatives. Tell them what your limits are in terms of talking about the death. Ask not to be contacted or to be contacted through an attorney or specially appointed advocate. If you clearly spell out your preferred boundaries, most people in the media will respect them. If they don't, you might need to consult legal authorities regarding your rights.

CARPE DIEM
If you are still receiving media inquiries about the death, appoint someone to handle them. This could be a family member, a friend of the family, or an attorney.

29.

KEEP IN MIND THE RULE OF THIRDS

"Grief rewrites your address book."
— Unknown

- In our own grief journeys and in the lives of the mourners I (Alan) have been privileged to counsel, we have discovered that in general, you can take all the people in your life and divide them into thirds when it comes to grief support.

- One third of the people in your life will turn out to be truly empathetic helpers. They will have a desire to understand you and your unique thoughts and feelings about the death. They will be willing to be involved in your pain and suffering without feeling the need to take it away from you. They will believe in your capacity to heal.

- Another third of the people in your life will turn out to be neutral in response to your grief. They will neither help nor hinder you in your journey.

- And the final third of people in your life will turn out to be harmful to you in your efforts to mourn and heal. While they are usually not intentionally setting out to harm you, they will judge you, try to take your grief away from you, and pull you off the path to healing.

- Seek out the friends and family members who fall into the first group. They will be your confidants and momentum-givers on your journey. When you are actively mourning, try to avoid the last group, for they will trip you up and cause you to fall.

CARPE DIEM
Get together for coffee or dinner with someone in the first third today.

30.

BE HONEST WITH THE CHILDREN WHO MOURN

"Live so that when your children think of fairness and integrity, they think of you."

— H. Jackson Brown

- Children are often forgotten mourners. We try to protect them from painful realities by not being open and honest with them. We hide our own grief because we don't want them to feel bad.

- Children can cope with what they know. They cannot cope with what they don't know or have never been told. When we're not honest or clear with them, they typically imagine circumstances even worse than the truth of the death.

- Children are amazing, resilient creatures. Tell them the truth. Use language they'll understand, but avoid euphemisms. Don't tell them Daddy went to sleep or God took Daddy. Learn to use the words "death" and "died." Explain the circumstances of the death, as well.

- Typically children require information in "doses." You may not need to explain every detail to them all at once. Let them come to you with questions as they're ready.

- Model your own grief for the children in your life. It's OK to let them see you cry and get upset.

- One of the most loving things you can do for children touched by traumatic death is get them help outside the family. When a family has been affected by traumatic death, you'll often see what I (Alan) call the "pressure cooker phenomenon." Typically everyone in the family has a high need to feel understood yet a low capacity to be understanding. If this is the case, seek help for the children from friends and professional caregivers.

CARPE DIEM

If a child is mourning this death, get him in to see a good counselor. She will give you some reassurance that you are doing what you can to help the child. TAPS offers a Good Grief Camp for children and youth as well as connections to grief counseling.

31.

IF YOU ARE GRIEVING WHAT WILL NEVER BE, SHARE THESE THOUGHTS AND FEELINGS

"I grieve for all the tomorrows that will never be.
I grieve because God now holds you instead of me."
—Unknown

- Because it is usually young people who die military-related deaths, the families who are left behind often end up grieving what will never be. Many service members die before they marry/form a significant relationship, have any children, or complete their own families.

- Surviving partners may have wanted children with the person who died and now it is too late. Others have children who will never know the mother or father who died. Grieving parents mourn the wedding or grandchildren they will never have the joy of experiencing.

- Grieving a lost future is normal and necessary. After all, when someone loved dies, you have not only lost the present with this person, you have lost the future you imagined. And when it is a young person who died, that imagined future included decades of love, laughter, and joy. That's a lot to lose.

- As with all thoughts and feelings in grief, sharing your loss of a hoped-for future is what will help you find ways to create a new, albeit different, future. Talk to people who care about you. Be open and honest with others grieving this death.

CARPE DIEM
Today, tell someone the one thing that makes you saddest
about the future without the person who died.

32.

KNOW THAT YOU ARE LOVED

"The true soldier fights not because he hates what is in front of him,
but because he loves what is behind him."
— G. K. Chesterton

- As Jane Howard wisely observed, "Call it a clan, call it a network, call it a tribe, call it a family. Whatever you call it, whoever you are, you need one." Yes, love from family, friends, and community gives life meaning and purpose. Look around for expressions of care and concern. These are people who love you and want to be an important part of your support system.

- Some of those who love you may not know how to reach out to you, but they still care about you. Reflect on those people and the ways in which your life matters to them. Open your heart and have gratitude for those who love you.

- Feeling connected to people around you can be a great source of joy and a cause for celebration. When you reach out to others, and they to you, you remember you are loved even during days of darkness and grief.

- In contrast, if you lose this connection, you suffer alone and in isolation. Feeling pessimistic, you may retreat even more. You begin to sever your relationships and make your world smaller. Over-isolation anchors your loss and sadness in place.

- You are connected to your family, friends, and community in a circle, with no end and no beginning. When you allow yourself to be a part of that circle, you find your place. You realize you belong and are a vital part of a bigger whole.

CARPE DIEM
Get out some notes and cards you have received from people who care about you. Re-read them and remind yourself that you are loved. Then, call someone you love and express gratitude that he is in your life.

33.

EXPRESS YOUR SPIRITUALITY

*"At any moment you have a choice that either leads you
closer to your spirit or further away from it."*
— Thich Nhat Hanh

- Above all, mourning is a spiritual journey of the heart and soul. Grief and loss invite you to consider why people live, why people die, and what gives life meaning and purpose. These are the most spiritual questions we have language to form.

- You can embrace your spirituality in many ways and through many practices—prayer, worship, and meditation among them. You can nurture your spirituality in many places—nature, church, temple, mosque, monastery, retreat center, or kitchen table.

- No one can "give" you spirituality from the outside in. Even when you take spiritual understanding and direction from a specific faith tradition, your understanding is uniquely yours, discovered through self-examination, reflection, and spiritual transformation.

CARPE DIEM

If you attend a place of worship or a spot where you feel closer to
God, visit it today, either for services or an informal time of prayer
and solitude. If you don't have such a place, perhaps you have a friend
who seems spiritually grounded. Ask her how she learned to nurture her
spirituality. Sometimes, someone else's ideas and practices provide just
what you need to stimulate your own spiritual self-care.

34.

IDENTIFY THREE PEOPLE YOU CAN TURN TO ANYTIME YOU NEED A FRIEND

"A friend is one who walks in when others walk out."
— Walter Winchell

- You may have many people who care about you but few who are able to be good companions in grief.

- Identify three people whom you think can be there for you in the coming months and years. Realize that the grief process can be long and arduous and that you mainly need to spend time with them and to be able to talk to them freely.

- Don't assume that others will help. Even normally compassionate people sometimes find it hard to be present to others in grief, especially in cases of sudden, violent death.

CARPE DIEM
Call these three people and ask them outright:
Will you please help me with my grief?
Tell them what you may need in the near and not-so-near future.

35.

RESET YOUR CLOCK

*"I know this much: that there is objective time, but also subjective time,
the kind you wear on the inside of your wrist, next to where
your pulse lies. And this personal time, which is the true time, is
measured in your relationship to memory."*
— Julian Barnes

- When someone you love dies suddenly, it seems as if your life is immediately divided into "Before" and "After." There is your life Before the traumatic death, and now there is your life After. It's as if your internal calendar gets reset to mark the significance of such a profound loss.

- Many traumatized grievers can tell you, seemingly without thought or conscious calculation, how many years, months, and days it has been since their loved one died.

- These new ways of keeping time are perfectly normal. You are not crazy! Your mind and heart have simply come up with a new system to mark Earth's relentless rotation.

- It's also OK to mention your new timekeeping system in everyday conversation: "Thanksgiving's coming. My son died four Thanksgivings ago." "Tomorrow would have been our fifth wedding anniversary." "Now I'm older than my brother was when he died." Comments such as these let others know that it's important to you to remember and to continue to tell the story.

CARPE DIEM
Write two columns on a piece of paper: Before and After.
In ten minutes, brainstorm as many adjectives or feelings that you can
think of that define each time period.

36.

LEAN ON—AND BEWARE OF— YOUR RESILIENCE

"To share your weakness is to make yourself vulnerable; to make yourself vulnerable is to show your strength."

— Criss Jami

- Military families are usually quite resilient. After all, military service is unpredictable. You may have had to pick up and move a number of times, forcing you to leave old friends and make new ones and re-establish community connections. Deployments are also unpredictable, and you may have been separated from your loved one for long stretches of time. Through all this, and because of the military's resilient culture, military families learn to roll with the punches.

- Your resilience training can help you right now. The most profound change that you could ever experience has happened, and now, as always, you've got to pick yourself up, dust yourself off, and keep putting one foot in front of the other. Your resilience can help you with practical matters such as relocating. It may also give you the knowledge that you will survive.

- When it comes to grief, it's also wise to beware of your learned resilience. It may tell you to "suck it up" and put your loss behind you. It may suggest that you need to be strong and in control. Yet what you actually need is to embrace your thoughts and feelings and give them the time and attention they deserve. What you need to do is relinquish control to your grief.

- Marshal your resilience in service of your grief. If you do the hard work of mourning (needs one through six), your resilience can remind you that you are strong enough to do things like embrace the pain of the loss and accept support from others.

CARPE DIEM

Identify the one way in which you are most resilient. How can it help you— and how could it actually hurt you—during the coming months?

37.

USE THE NAME OF THE PERSON WHO DIED

"Everyone is always telling me to listen to my heart,
but all it's saying is your name."
— Unknown.

- When you're talking about the death or about your life in general, don't avoid using the name of the person who died. Using the name lets others know they can use it, too.

- Acknowledge the significance of the life and your ongoing love by talking about the person who died: "I remember when Jesse . . .", "I was thinking of Sarah today because . . ."

- Encourage your friends and family to use the name of the person who died, too. We know we love to hear the names of the people in our lives who have died. How about you?

CARPE DIEM
Flip through a baby name book at a local bookstore or online
and look up the name of the person who died. Reflect on the name's
meaning as it relates to the person you loved.

38.

TURN TO YOUR FAMILY

"You don't choose your family.
They are God's gift to you, as you are to them."
— Desmond Tutu

- In today's mobile, disconnected society, many people have lost touch with the gift of family. This can be especially true for military people because you are often stationed far away from your hometowns. Yet, remember this: Your friends may come and go, but family, as they say, is forever.

- If you're emotionally close to members of your family, you're probably already reaching out to them for support. Allow them to be there for you. Let them in.

- If you're not emotionally close to your family, perhaps now is the time to open closed doors. Call a family member you haven't spoken to for a while. Hop in a car or on a plane and make a long overdue visit.

- Don't feel bad if you have to be the initiator; instead, expend your energy by writing that first letter or making that first phone call.

- On the other hand, you probably know some family members you should keep your distance from. They may be among the one-third who are bound to make you feel worse (see Idea 29). Remember, sometimes you can love someone even though you don't like them or feel you can count on them for support, compassion, and understanding.

CARPE DIEM
Call a family member you feel close to today.
Make plans to visit this person soon.

39.

TURN TO SOCIAL MEDIA TO HELP YOU MOURN

*"At times, we are the bridge that allows another
to re-enter the world after a loss."*
— Danielle Pierre

- Social sites like Facebook and Twitter can be supportive gathering places for families after a military death.

- Sharing news, advice, and empathetic words with friends and family, including others who have experienced a military loss, may help you feel understood and less alone.

- Remember your mourning needs. Participating in social media can help you with all six.

- On Facebook, you can create a memorial page for the person who died, or you can convert his or her existing Facebook to a memorial page. This then becomes a location for news of the death and other updates as well as a perpetual spot for mourners to gather, share memories and photos, and support one another.

- But, a caution: If social media ever starts to feel more like a burden or a drain than an asset, step away from it for a while. You don't have to delete the accounts. You can simply ignore them for a time. They'll be there if and when you want to return.

CARPE DIEM
If you haven't already, look into setting up a memorial page on
Facebook for the person who died.

40.

ORGANIZE A MEMORY BOOK

"Sharing tales of those we've lost is how we keep from really losing them."
— Mitch Albom

• Assembling a scrapbook that holds treasured photos and mementos of the person who died can be a very helpful activity.

• You might consider including a birth certificate, schoolwork, newspaper clippings, locks of hair, old letters, military communications or commendations, the obituary—anything that helps tell the story of this unique and precious life.

• Phone others who loved the person who died and ask them to write a note or contribute photos.

• Other ideas: a memory box, photo buttons of the person who died (nice for a younger person), a memory quilt.

CARPE DIEM
Buy an appropriate scrapbook or keepsake box today. Don't forget
to buy the associated materials you'll need, such as photo
pages or photo corners, glue, scissors, etc.

41.

EMBRACE THE IMAGE OF THE EAGLE

"The eagle, full of the boundless spirit of freedom, living above the valleys, strong and powerful in his might, has become the national emblem of a country that offers freedom in word and thought and an opportunity for a full and free expansion into the boundless space of the future."

— Maude M. Grant

- The eagle is not only the national bird of the United States, it is also a proud military insignia. In addition, the image of the eagle is found across a broad range of spiritual beliefs and philosophies. Depending on the tradition, it symbolizes strength, courage, wisdom, spiritual protection, and healing.

- The eagle's soaring flight has drawn comparisons to the Holy Spirit, intuition, and grace.

- Some native cultures believe that the eagle carries our prayers to the Creator. There is a Native American blessing that says:

May you have the strength
Of eagles' wings,
The faith and courage to
Fly to new heights,
And the wisdom
Of the universe
To carry you there.

- If you are moved by the sight of eagles, frame a photo of one or buy a piece of eagle artwork and place it somewhere you will see it often.

CARPE DIEM
Listen to the song "On Eagles Wings" by Michael Joncas. Talk with a trusted friend about what this bring up for you.

42.

IF YOU FEEL ANGRY, FIND APPROPRIATE WAYS TO EXPRESS YOUR ANGER

"Anger is a symptom, a way of cloaking and expressing feelings too awful to experience directly—hurt, bitterness, grief, and, most of all, fear."
— Joan Rivers

- It's normal to feel intensely angry after a death, especially when you perceive that someone may be at fault or contributed in some way to the cause of the death. You may obsess over your feelings of rage and hate toward those responsible. In cases of accidental death, you may be mad at God or at the vagaries of fate that led your loved one to be in the wrong place at the wrong time.

- Logically or illogically, you may also feel angry with others. You may be mad at someone in your family for their response to the death or at your best friend because she has not suffered as you have. It's also common for mourners of military death to feel, as part of a mixture of emotions, anger at the person who died. How could you abandon me? Why did you have to be in that place at that time? Why did you choose the military over your family?

- Anger is normal and necessary. It's our way of protesting a reality we don't like. It helps us survive. It also helps counter more passive, painful feelings, such as despair and sadness.

- Like all your feelings, anger is not wrong. It simply is. What you *do* with your anger can be wrong, however. Never harm yourself or someone else in an attempt to squelch your rage. Instead, express your anger in appropriate ways. Talk about it. Vent it to someone who can listen without feeling attacked. Write it down. Share it in the safety of a support group. Use the extra energy to clean the house, exercise, or do a chore you have not had the time or gumption to tackle.

CARPE DIEM
Today, do something physical to vent your anger. Go for a fast walk or punch a pillow. Smash a tennis ball against a practice wall over and over.

43.

IF YOU FEEL GUILTY OR REGRETFUL, FIND WAYS TO EXPRESS IT

"Guilt is perhaps the most painful companion of death."
— Coco Chanel

- Sometimes military deaths give rise to feelings of guilt or regret in survivors.

- Battle buddies often feel guilty when one of their own dies, especially if it was on what they consider "their watch." Spouses may feel regret about things that were said (or weren't said) or guilty about their own behavior in some way. Parents may feel guilty if they encouraged their child to enlist or continue service or even if they were unable to dissuade him.

- It's natural to feel guilt and regret after a sudden, untimely death. We all wonder how we could have prevented it. We all harbor feelings of unfinished business. We all wish we could have a "do over."

- If you feel guilt and regret, find ways to explore these feelings. Most of the time, we are not actually responsible for contributing to the death or any mistakes other than those that come with the territory of being human, but we still need to share our guilt and regret outside of ourselves. When we express these feelings, when we expose them to the cold light of day, we often gain a better perspective. We see that although these feelings are normal and natural, we are good people. We can learn to forgive ourselves and practice self-compassion.

CARPE DIEM
If you feel strong guilt or regret, express these feelings today by talking to someone who does not judge or try to fix but who will instead listen and empathize.

44.

IF YOU FEEL STUCK, FIND WAYS TO GET UNSTUCK

"Growth is painful. Change is painful. But nothing is as painful as staying stuck somewhere you don't belong."
— Mandy Hale

- Sometimes people in grief feel stuck. They may feel like they can't shake a certain aspect of their grief. They might constantly feel dazed, depressed, angry, disorganized, lethargic, or any number of feelings. They may obsess for weeks over a certain thought or idea.

- In grief, there's a concept I (Alan) like to teach about called "perturbation." After a loss, when you are honest and open about your grief and work to actively mourn—you create movement. Another way to say this is that mourning puts your emotions in motion. I use the term "perturbation" to refer to this capacity to experience change and movement. To integrate grief, you must be touched by what you experience *and* you must express what you experience. If you do not allow yourself to feel what you are feeling and/or if you do not express what you are feeling, you can't be changed by it. Instead, you may well become "stuck."

- Being stuck in grief usually means that you need to find more effective ways to express whatever it is you feel stuck about. Talk to others about it. Write about it in a journal. Share it in a support group. See a competent grief counselor about it. Keep trying different approaches until you shake it loose.

- Don't expect to reconcile your grief quickly. It will likely take many months and years to move through even your most acute symptoms of grief. But in the long-term, don't assume that your stuck condition is "just the way it is." You can get unstuck! Ask for help.

CARPE DIEM
If you feel stuck about something, talk to someone about it today.

45.

KNOW THAT IT'S OK NOT TO FORGIVE

"To make the right choices in life, you have to get in touch with your soul."
— Deepak Chopra

- Military deaths usually result from the acts of others. In combat, people on opposing sides kill one another with full intention. Yet sometimes military deaths are accidental. Someone may have accidentally killed or contributed to the death of the person you love.

- The rules of your religion may ask you to forgive those who are to blame—whether they are the people directly responsible or others who may bear indirect responsibility, such as the officers in charge—who put your loved one in harm's way. Or you may simply believe that you *should* forgive, that you are a lesser or bad person if you are unable to forgive.

- Forgiveness is not necessary for healing. For some survivors, forgiveness is an important milestone in their journeys through grief; they feel relieved of a heavy burden. For others, heartfelt forgiveness is not to be. If this applies to you, does this mean you're "stuck" in your grief journey or that you'll never truly heal? Not necessarily. It simply means you have come to a decision about the morality of the death. This decision, forgiving or unforgiving, is part of your grief.

- In cases of suicide, forgiveness is an even more complex issue. Can you forgive someone you love for taking herself from you? Can you forgive yourself and others who, on the look back, wish they had done something different? While you may never agree with the act of suicide, active mourning—including time, education, and compassionate support—can help you make peace with the act.

CARPE DIEM
If this issue is weighing on your mind, it may help you to talk to someone about what forgiveness or lack of forgiveness means to you. Explore it with a good listener. Express your thoughts and feelings.

46.

BREATHE

"Feelings come and go like clouds in a windy sky.
Conscious breathing is my anchor."
— Thich Nhat Hanh

- When the demands of your grief—not to mention the demands of your daily life—feel overwhelming, stop what you're doing for a few minutes and just breathe.

- If you can, give yourself five full minutes to concentrate on your breathing. Breathe from your diaphragm: push your belly out as you breathe in and pull your belly in as you breathe out. Imagine that you're inhaling the spiritual energy you need to heal and that you're exhaling your sadness and bad feelings.

- Breathing opens you up. Grief may have closed you down. The power of breath helps to fill your empty spaces. The old wisdom of "count to ten" is all about taking a breath to open up space for something else to happen.

- Meditate if meditation helps center you. Find someplace quiet, be still, close your eyes, and focus on breathing in and out. Relax your muscles. Listen to your own heartbeat. When you notice yourself thinking about something other than your breathing, gently let the thought go and bring your attention back to your breath.

- Consciously breathe in and out; you can slow the world down and touch the edges of your true self.

CARPE DIEM
Sit down, focus on something 10 feet away, and take 20 deep breaths.

47.

WORK THROUGH FINANCIAL STRESSES

"Never refuse to give help when it is needed...
nor refuse to accept it when it is offered."
— Lloyd Alexander

- Military deaths can cause financial difficulties on top of the emotional and spiritual stresses. Even after death benefits and other military support are received, lost work time, childcare, relocation or travel costs, and other expenses can all contribute to financial overload.

- If you were the beneficiary of the Death Gratuity or the SGLI benefit, your feelings about the money can be an additional stressor. It's hard not to consider these payouts as blood money, and some survivors find it difficult to actually use the money, since its use would signify that the loved one truly is dead.

- If you or your family is under financial stress right now, ask for help. Ask someone you trust to take charge of your finances right now so you can concentrate on your grief.

- Make sure you are receiving all the military benefits you are owed (see Idea 68). Check with your Casualty Assistance Officer if you have questions or benefits. Call TAPS and ask for the free Benefits and Finances guide.

- Whatever you do, don't ignore your finances right now. Delinquencies and defaulting on loans will only cause you bigger headaches in the months to come.

CARPE DIEM

Among your friends and family, who's the best financial
manager you know? Ask this person to step in and help you with money
issues for the next several months. Remember—reaching out for and
accepting help is one of your mourning needs.

48.

WRITE A LETTER

"To send a letter is a good way to go somewhere
without moving anything but your heart."
— Phyllis Theroux

- Sometimes articulating our thoughts and feelings in letter form helps us understand them better.

- Write a letter to the person who died telling her how you feel now that she's gone. Consider the following prompts:
  - What I miss most about you is…
  - What I wish I'd said or hadn't said is…
  - What's hardest for me now is…
  - What I'd like to ask you is…
  - I'm keeping my memories of you alive by…

  Read your letter aloud at the cemetery or to a photo of the person who died.

- Another healing exercise can be writing a letter to yourself on behalf of the person who died. Imagine that the person who died is writing you from heaven. What would he say to you? How would he want you to live the rest of your life?

- Write a letter to God telling him how you feel about the death.

- Write thank you notes to helpers such as neighbors, funeral directors, medics, or other service members who tried to help or were close to the person who died, etc.

CARPE DIEM
Write a letter to someone you love who's still alive telling
her why she's so important to you.

49.

DEAL WITH PERSONAL EFFECTS IN YOUR OWN TIME

"I walk down memory lane because I know I'll run into you there."
— Unknown

- If you receive your loved one's footlocker or boxes of personal effects, we understand how hard it can be to open them and sort through all the contents.

- You don't have to hurry. As with all things in grief, there is no reward for speed. Go through your loved one's belongings if and when you're ready. You may want to leave personal items untouched for months or sometimes years.

- You may be comforted by physical objects that belonged to or were associated with the person who died. You may save clothing, jewelry, military tokens such as dog tags, locks of hair, and other personal items. Such "linking objects" can help you remember the person who died and honor the life that was lived. Such objects can help you heal. Never think that being attached to these objects is morbid or wrong.

- Have a quilt made from your loved one's military uniforms or favorite shirts and snuggle up with it on chilly evenings to keep yourself warm. If you are able to part with some of your loved one's possessions, offer mementos, clothes, or books to other family members who would cherish them.

- Watch out for people who try to tell you that if you force yourself to get rid of linking objects, it will help you "accept" the loss. These people may be well-intentioned, but they are sadly misinformed.

CARPE DIEM

When and only when you're ready, ask a friend or family member to help you sort through the personal belongings of the person who died. Fill a memory box with significant objects and mementos.

50.

SHARE YOUR DREAMS ABOUT THE PERSON WHO DIED

"I think we dream so we don't have to be apart so long. If we're in each other's dreams, we can play together all night."
— Bill Watterson

- Mourners often dream about the person who died. This is a normal response to loss and grief.

- You may have dreams that are upsetting, even violent. You may dream about the circumstances of the death. You may dream that you are there when the death occurs (but still helpless to prevent it). You may have seemingly unrelated nightmares. These dreams are your mind's way of attempting to process the reality of the death.

- If you are consistently having nightmares since the death, we strongly suggest you see a professional grief counselor. You deserve to get help to understand what you might be able to do to convert your nightmares into dreams.

- On the other hand, you may have very happy, reassuring dreams about the person who died. You may even feel you have been "visited" by him in your dreams. Perhaps he has told you that he's OK and that you'll be OK too.

- It's also normal NOT to dream about the death or the person who died. You may be sleeping poorly and thus not dreaming in your normal pattern. Or you may be having dreams but not remembering them.

CARPE DIEM

Talking about your dreams—whether they're happy or sad—is another way to express your grief. Or you might consider starting a "dream journal" in which you record your dreams as soon as you wake up.

51.

PRAY

*"Through prayer, you can enjoy the fellowship of Heaven
and walk in it throughout the day."*
— Roy Lessin

- In a sense, prayer is mourning because prayer means taking your feelings and articulating them to someone else. Even when you pray silently, you're forming words for your thoughts and feelings and you're offering up those words to a presence outside yourself.

- Someone wise once noted, "Our faith is capable of reaching the realm of mystery."

- Did you know that real medical studies have shown that prayer can actually help people heal?

- If you believe in a higher power, pray. Pray for the person who died. Pray for your questions about life and death to be answered. Pray for the strength to embrace your pain and to go on to find continued meaning in life and living. Pray for others affected by this death.

- Many places of worship have prayer lists. Call and ask that your name be added to the prayer list. On worship days, the whole congregation will pray for you. Often many individuals will pray at home for those on the prayer list, as well.

CARPE DIEM
Bow your head right now and say a silent prayer. If you are out of practice, don't worry; just let your thoughts flow naturally.

52.

DON'T STRESS ABOUT THANK-YOU NOTES

"Don't sweat the small stuff...and it's all small stuff."
— Richard Carlson

- When we are in mourning, we need to practice self-compassion. We need to be kind and gentle with ourselves. If you're someone who believes that it's necessary to write thank-you notes to those who have gifted you with food, donations, or other kindnesses since the death, we want to remind you: it's OK to do whatever you need to do to survive right now.

- If writing thank-you notes helps you feel better or do your grief work, then by all means, write them. But if the idea of writing all those thank-you notes fills you with guilt or despair, let it go. The people who care about you understand that you've got more important things than thank-you notes to worry about right now.

- Some alternatives to individual, handwritten thank-you notes include: a generic group email or social media post; notes written on your behalf by a friend who wants to help in some way; cards sent months from now, maybe when the holidays roll around; simple, quick texts you send on your phone; nothing.

CARPE DIEM
If tardy thank-you notes are stressing you out and you can't give yourself permission to let them go, talk to a friend or family member about them today. Ask for help.

53.

VISIT THE CEMETERY

"Peace to each manly soul that sleepeth;
Rest to each faithful eye that weepeth."
— Thomas Moore

- Visiting the cemetery is an important mourning ritual. It helps us embrace our loss and remember the person who died.

- Memorial Day, Veteran's Day, Labor Day, Mother's Day, or Father's Day are traditional days to visit the cemetery and pay respects.

- If the body was cremated, you may want to visit the scattering site or columbarium.

- Even if your loved one wasn't buried in a military cemetery, you might want to go out of your way to visit one some day. Seeing your loved one's death in the context of so much patriotic sacrifice is a stirring experience.

- Ask a friend or family member to go with you. You may feel comforted by their presence. Or, if you are like me (Alan), you may find it more meaningful to visit the cemetery alone. Do what feels right for you.

CARPE DIEM
If you can, drop by the cemetery today with fresh flowers.
Scatter the petals over the grave.

54.

WEAR YOUR STORY

"She had been proud of his decision to serve his country,
her heart bursting with love and admiration the first time
she saw him outfitted in his dress blues."
— Nicholas Sparks

- Your loved one wore a uniform as part of his service in the military. Wear symbols of his sacrifice if it brings you comfort.

- Many military survivors make an American flag pin part of their everyday dress. Your loved one swore an oath to protect and defend that flag, and one draped their casket. You have earned a special right to wear one with pride if you choose.

- If you received a Gold Star lapel pin or Next of Kin Deceased pin from the casualty officer, wear it as a symbol of your loss in the military. TAPS also offers a pin engraved with images of a folded flag, bugler, and military flyover. Wearing these allows others to know that you are part of the national military family that has sacrificed for their freedom.

- Have a memorial bracelet made, engraved with your loved one's rank, name, and dates of life and service. When you are asked about the bracelet, this will give you an opportunity to talk about your loved one.

- There may be uniform items, like a flight jacket or cap, that belonged to your loved one that you can wear to feel closer to them.

CARPE DIEM
Find those symbols of your loved one's service, your patriotism, or your connection to organizations supporting military surviving families and wear them. You are not alone; you are part of a community of loving care.

55.

EXAMINE OLD HURTS

*"We all make mistakes, have struggles, and even regret things
in our past. But…you are here NOW with the power to
shape your day and your future."*
— Steve Maraboli

- When someone we love dies suddenly and unexpectedly, we often find ourselves hurting over unfinished business or unhealed wounds.

- In the military, deployments often separate service members from their loved ones for long periods of time. During those lengthy deployments, we usually can't communicate with one another very thoroughly. The lack of communication may cause hurts and misunderstandings to pile up. Then, when the service member is on leave, we might set aside the hurt pile in order not to ruin what little time we have together. And now…now it's too late.

- If you carry old hurts from your relationship with the person who died, they are now part of your grief. And if they are bothering you, it means you need to take a look at them and talk them out with someone.

- It's funny how sometimes little slights or hiccups from the past can give us more heartache than seemingly large problems. Listen to your heart. If it tells you that something doesn't matter and your heart is at peace with it, then you probably don't need to dredge it up and re-examine it. But if it's bugging you, if it gives you a little twinge of pain every time it floats to the surface, well then, bring it out into the open and let it run around.

CARPE DIEM
Make a list of things that are bothering you from your history
with the person who died. Pick one and talk about it today with
someone who's a good listener (or write about it in your journal).

56.

GATHER NEW MEMORIES OF THE PERSON WHO DIED

"Memories are the key not to the past, but to the future."
— Corrie Ten Boom

• You can no longer create new firsthand memories of time spent with the person who died. That is a painful reality to acknowledge and embrace.

• But you *can* gather memories from others who knew and cared about your special person. The more you ask them to share their memories, the more likely that you'll be gifted with memories that are new to *you*.

• Talk with or write to your loved one's childhood friends, teachers, and neighbors. Strike up conversations with fellow service members or past civilian coworkers. Tell them you're on a mission to collect new memories—for yourself and perhaps also for other friends and family members who are hurting.

• Consider jotting down notes in a special notebook you designate for this purpose. Or ask permission to record the conversations with a simple, free audio app on your phone.

• Be prepared to hear stories that evoke happiness and love as well as anger, sadness, regret, and other challenging emotions. Gather up all of the new memories and savor them. They are precious.

CARPE DIEM
Start your new memory hunt today. Send a group email asking friends and family each to submit one special memory.

57.

BEFRIEND EIGHT UNIVERSAL
HEALING PRINCIPLES

"Balance is not something you find. It's something you create."
— Jana Kingsford

- Eight healing principles, used in the majority of cultures, can help sustain your physical, emotional, cognitive, social, and spiritual well-being. Explore the list below and note which of the universal principles you are embracing and which you are neglecting.

SUPPORT HEALTH AND WELL-BEING	NON-SUPPORTIVE OF HEALTH AND WELL-BEING
Balanced diet	Unbalanced diet
Daily and weekly exercise	Lack of exercise
Time for fun, play, and laughter	Lack of humor, fun, and play
Enjoying music	Lack of music
Love, touch, and support systems	Lack of love, touch, and support systems
Engaged in interests, hobbies, and creative purposes	Lack of interests, hobbies, and creative purposes
Nature, beauty, and healing environments	Lack of nature, beauty, and healing environments
Faith and belief in the supernatural	Lack of faith and belief in the supernatural

- These eight principles can guide you as you move through the pain of grief towards healing and balance in your life. Because mind, body, and spirit are closely connected, by working through your unbalanced areas you will help soothe the tension within your body and allow healing of your entire being.

CARPE DIEM:
Make a commitment to rebalance those areas that are not supportive to your overall well-being. Get out a piece of paper right now and write out an "action plan for creating balance."

58.

BE AWARE OF "GRIEF OVERLOAD"

"When it rains, it pours."

- Unfortunately, sometimes people (maybe you) experience more than one loss in a short period of time. In the military, a single combat or training mission gone wrong can result in many deaths. In your civilian life, other losses may coincidentally follow on the heels of the military death.

- Other types of losses—job changes, divorce, illness, children leaving home—can also occur on top of death loss. And a military death often sets other losses in motion—a housing and/or city relocation, a change in school for children, a loss of income or stability.

- When multiple losses happen around the same time, you may be at risk for "grief overload." Your ability to cope may be stretched beyond its limits. You might feel torn, grieving one loss this minute and another the next. You might feel like you're going crazy.

- Rest assured, you're not going crazy. You are, however, in need of special care. If you're grief overloaded, you must try to figure out ways to cope with all the stress yet still find the time and focus you need to grieve and mourn. Reach out to others for help. You cannot get through this alone. See a counselor, if only to help you survive the roughest patches. Join a support group. Start a grief journal. Be proactive in getting help for yourself.

- Fertile soil that produces healthy growth does so because it has been well-tended in the early cycles of the planting season. This is also true with our grief.

CARPE DIEM
If you're grief overloaded right now, sit down and make a list of
five things you can do right now to help offload some of your stress. Make
it a point to take action on them today.

59.

ESTABLISH A MEMORIAL FOR THE PERSON WHO DIED

"A hero is someone who has given his or her life to something bigger than oneself."
— Joseph Campbell

• Sometimes grieving families ask that memorial contributions be made to specified charities in the name of the person who died. This practice allows friends and family members to show their support while helping the family feel that something good came of the death.

• You can establish a personalized and ongoing memorial to the person who died, even if it has been some time since the death.

• What was meaningful to the person who died? Did she support a certain nonprofit or participate in a certain recreational activity? What did she most care about in life?

• Your local bank or funeral home may have ideas about how to go about setting up a memorial fund. Or you might work with your community to establish a memorial garden, park, or monument. You might even consider working toward having a street, bridge, or building named for your loved one.

CARPE DIEM
Call someone else who loves the person who died and together brainstorm a list of ideas for a memorial. Suggest that both of you commit to making at least one additional phone call for information before the day is out.

60.

BE THE HERO

"The brave may not live forever, but the cautious do not live at all."
— Unknown

- In many ways, those who serve in the military are our heroes. They serve and protect us. They are brave and selfless. They put their own needs—and lives—after the lives of their countrymen and women.

- Their heroism places them in harm's way, of course, and sometimes our military heroes die. When they die, we grieve and we must mourn. We have been talking about the need and ways to mourn throughout this book.

- But mourning takes courage. It's challenging to step up and embrace and express your pain. It hurts, and it's scary. But the person you loved was a hero. You, too, can be a hero by mustering the courage to mourn openly and honestly.

- When you're the hero of your own grief journey, you're not only helping yourself heal—you're honoring your loved one's heroism. He mustered the courage to serve. Now you can muster the courage to mourn.

CARPE DIEM
The next time you are afraid of the grief inside you, remember your loved one's bravery. If she was a hero, couldn't you be a hero, too?

61.

CRY

"There is a sacredness in tears. They are not a mark of weakness, but of power. They speak more eloquently than ten thousand tongues. They are the messengers of overwhelming grief, of deep contrition, and of unspeakable love."
— Washington Irving

- Tears are a natural cleansing and healing mechanism. They rid your body of stress chemicals. It's OK to cry. In fact, it's good to cry when you feel like it. What's more, tears are a form of mourning. They are sacred!

- Your pain, your grief, your overwhelming loss disturbs the world around you. Disturb the quiet with your soul's cry.

- On the other hand, don't feel bad if you aren't crying a lot. Not everyone is a crier.

- You may find that those around you are uncomfortable with your tears. As a society, we're often not so good at witnessing others in pain. Don't let those people take your grief away from you.

- Explain to your friends and family that you need to cry right now and that they can help by allowing you to.

- As a traumatized griever, you may even find yourself keening, which means a loud wailing or wordless crying out in lament for the dead. Keening is an instinctive form of mourning. It gives voice to your profound pain at a time when words are inadequate.

- You may find yourself crying at unexpected times or places. If you need to, excuse yourself and retreat to somewhere private. Or better yet, go ahead and cry openly and honestly, unashamed of your tears of overwhelming grief.

CARPE DIEM
If you feel like it, have a good cry today. Find a safe place to embrace your pain, and cry as long and as hard as you want to.

62.

VISIT THE GREAT OUTDOORS

"By observing nature you begin to sense the harmonious interaction of all the elements and forces of life. Whether it be a stream, a forest, a mountain, or the sea, connecting with nature's intelligence will give you a sense of unity with all of life and help you to get in touch with the innermost essence of your being."

— Deepak Chopra

- For many people it is restorative and energizing to spend time outside.

- You may find nature's timeless beauty healing. The sound of a bird singing or the awesome presence of an old tree can help put things in perspective. Rediscover what it feels like to walk barefoot in the grass or the sand and breathe the fresh air. Mother Earth knows more about kicking back than all the stress management experts on the planet— and she charges far less.

- Go on a nature walk. Or camping. Or canoeing. The farther away from civilization the better.

- I (Alan) remember a recent time when I was feeling overwhelmed and I just went for a walk. I saw beautiful flowers. I saw leaves falling from the trees. I watched my Husky dogs leap with joy. I took long, deep breaths. I felt a sense of gratitude. After the walk, I felt renewed, changed.

- TAPS offers restorative and therapeutic nature retreats for those grieving the death of a service member. Visit www.taps.org and click on Survivor Events for more information.

CARPE DIEM

Look up walking paths or hiking trails in your community that you've never tried before. Or go to the cemetery. Many contain walking paths and offer lovely settings and solitude. Take a walk today.

63.

TAKE A HEALING FIELD TRIP

"This trip changed my life. I got off the plane in Alaska knowing no one. I was really nervous, but there was Bonnie welcoming me with a warm hug. It was at that moment I knew this organization was something special, and by the end of the weekend I had a new family."

— A surviving TAPS fiancée

- In many ways and cases, the military experience is something that happens apart from the service member's friends and family. Basic training is far from home, and so are most deployments.

- But it's not too late to round out your understanding of the far-away people and places your loved one experienced.

- Consider visiting the base where your loved one attended basic training. Ask for a tour and try to meet training officers and others who may remember your loved one.

- In her book *After the Flag Has Been Folded: A Daughter Remembers the Father She Lost to War*, Karen Spears Zacharias describes how, years after his death, she traveled to Vietnam to see for herself where he had fought and what he had fought for. Her trip gave her a perspective and peace she could get in no other way. You, too, might be able to make a pilgrimage to the site of your loved one's deployment and death once it becomes a safe travel destination. Often, the reality is much more normal, even comforting, than we imagine it to be. If possible, place a marker where the death occurred.

- You might also find it healing to visit non-military sites from your loved one's past, such as his place of birth or old high school.

CARPE DIEM
Talk with your family about the places you want to visit.
See if anyone else would like to go with you. Make plans.

64.

REMEMBER OTHERS WHO HAD A SPECIAL RELATIONSHIP WITH THE PERSON WHO DIED

"Come with me and know that we are all a family circle, broken by death but mended by love."

— Darcie Sims

- At times your appropriately inward focus will make you feel alone in your grief. But you're not alone. There are many other people who love and miss the person who died.

- Think about others who were affected by your loved one's death: parents, children, siblings, friends, neighbors, distant relatives, battle buddies.

- After a death, the primary mourners receive sympathy and attention. Is there someone outside the main circle who nonetheless had a close relationship or history with the person and may be struggling with the death? Perhaps you could call her and invite her out for coffee.

- Give a gift to one of these people. If you have extras of your loved one's insignia, consider offering them to those who were close to the person who died as a way they can carry your loved one's legacy forward.

CARPE DIEM
Call someone else today who may be having a hard time with this death.

65.

LAUGH

*"Coffee tastes better if the latrines are dug
downstream from an encampment."*
— U.S. Army Field Regulations, 1861

- Humor is one of the most healing gifts of humanity. Laughter restores hope and assists us in surviving the pain of grief. It helps us feel peace in both mind and body.

- Don't fall into the trap of thinking that laughing means you don't miss the person who died. Laughing doesn't mean you are not in mourning.

- Sometimes it helps to think about what the person who died would want for you. Wouldn't she want you to laugh and continue to find joy in life, even in the midst of your sorrow?

- You can only embrace the pain of your loss a little at a time, in doses. In between the doses, it's perfectly normal, even necessary, to love and laugh.

- Remember the fun times you shared with the person who died. Remember his sense of humor. Remember his grin and the sound of his laughter.

- It has been said that laughter is a form of internal jogging. Not only is it enjoyable, it is good for you. Studies show that smiling, laughing, and feeling good enhance your immune system and make you healthier.

CARPE DIEM:
Close your eyes right now and try to remember the smile
and laughter of the person who died.

66.

BE AWARE OF HOW MILITARY PEOPLE AND PLACES AFFECT YOU

"Environment modifies life but does not govern life.
The soul is stronger than its surroundings."
— William James

- The military does a good job of setting itself apart from ordinary civilian life. The uniforms, the lingo, the expected behaviors, even the flag are all so powerfully symbolic that whenever you are around them, you are likely to be reminded of your loss.

- Remember, acknowledging and embracing the pain of your loss are two of your six needs of mourning. So being reminded of the death can be a helpful and healing experience.

- Spending time with your loved one's fellow service members or in places such as the commissary, veterans' memorials, or veterans' cemeteries may be part of your grief work. Whether you find comfort in them or ambivalence, anger, or other emotions (or most likely a combination of feelings), the military experience is central to your loved one's life and death. These people and places are part of the truth and therefore part of your grief work.

- On the other hand, if at times you are struggling with military reminders, it's OK to give yourself a break. As long as you continue to connect with the military now and then in ways you find meaningful, you will be coming to terms with your thoughts and feelings and moving toward reconciling them.

CARPE DIEM

Is there something you loved or respected about the military experience that you can carry with you, such as a photo that shows your loved one's pride on the day he finished basic training or officer training school, a medal, a note from a fellow service member, or a memento from a service member's family? Carry it with you in your wallet or purse. It can be your talisman if and when you find yourself struggling with the military nature of the death.

67.

BE A CIVVY

"Maybe the answer to Selective Service is to start everyone off in the Army and draft them for civilian life as needed."
— Bill Vaughn

- If you decide that you need to break rank from military people, places, and memories for a while, go out of your way to be completely civilian.

- In addition to avoiding those people and places for the time being, look closely at your own household and habits. Are you doing certain things in certain ways because of the military influence? If so, maybe you want to throw the rules out the window and do things differently for a bit.

- Talk to your civilian friends about their loss and healing experiences. Do they have any wisdom to offer?

- We're not suggesting that you cut all ties with the military or forget your pride in your loved one's service. We're just saying that in order to understand and appreciate something, sometimes you need to leave it for a while.

CARPE DIEM
What's the civviest thing you can think of doing today—
something you don't usually do? Give it a go.

68.

DISCOVER RESOURCES AVAILABLE TO SURVIVING MILITARY FAMILIES

"Thank you so much for your help with this matter.
You all take the time to research it for me and send me all of the
information I need. I really appreciate it because sometimes it is just too
much to handle without my husband around."

— A letter to TAPS from a survivor

- In addition to the dependency compensation, housing allowance, unpaid compensation, the Death Gratuity, SGLI, and Social Security death benefits you may have received, it's important to know about other benefits and resources you and your family may be eligible for as surviving family members of a military death.

- The Dependents' Educational Assistance (DEA) program provides up to 45 months of education benefits for degree or certificate programs, apprenticeships, or on-the-job training. Children are generally eligible from ages 18 to 26. Spouses are eligible for 10 years after the death or 20 years if the death happened during active duty. The VA also has scholarships for military survivors, as do many states and schools.

- Eligible spouses may also receive VA home loans, which offer better terms than other types of mortgages.

- As a surviving military family, you might also be eligible for educational and career counseling, financial counseling, commissary privileges, and civil service preference points.

CARPE DIEM

If you're unsure about which benefits you may be eligible for, call the VA toll-free at 1-800-827-1000. Call TAPS at 800-959-8277 to speak with someone in casework assistance and request the Education Support Services and Benefits and Finances guides. And remember that reaching out for and accepting help from others is one of your needs of mourning.

69.

PREPARE YOURSELF FOR THE HOLIDAYS

"Oh that it were possible,
After long grief and pain,
To find the arms of my true love
Around me once again."
— Alfred Lord Tennyson

- Because the person who died is no longer there to share the holidays with, you may feel particularly sad and vulnerable during Christmas, Hanukkah, and other holidays that are special to your family.

- Don't overextend yourself during the holidays. Don't feel you have to shop, bake, entertain, send cards, etc. if you're not up for it.

- Sometimes old holiday rituals are comforting after a death and sometimes they're not. Continue them only if they feel good to you; consider creating new ones, as well.

- Take inventory of who you want to spend holiday time with and who you don't. I (Alan) always try to keep in mind the "rule of thirds" (Idea 29). Try to seek out the last third and limit contact with the others.

- In addition to religious and family holidays, military survivors may find that patriotic holidays also leave them feeling vulnerable and sad. Try to prepare ahead for the sights and sounds of Memorial Day, Flag Day, Independence Day, and Veterans Day. The service branches also celebrate special days related to their inception. Others holidays to be on the lookout for: Inauguration Day, 9/11, Gold Star Mothers Day, and Pearl Harbor Day.

CARPE DIEM
What's the next major holiday? Make a game plan right now and let those you usually spend the day with know of your plan well in advance.

70.

CREATE A SANCTUARY JUST FOR YOU

"Reacquaint yourself with your spirit by slowing down and turning your focus inward. You will hear the whispered wisdom of your true self, which has long been forgotten and can now be remembered."
— Heather Stang

- Mourners need safe places where they can go when they feel ready to embrace their grief.

- Create a sanctuary in your own home, a retreat that's just for you. Furnish it with a comfy chair, reading materials, a journal, a music player. No TV or computer. Or, you may want this to be a room dedicated to silence. As Thomas Moore has noted, "Silence allows many sounds to reach awareness that otherwise would be unheard."

- Display photos of the person who died in your sanctuary if you think that will help you meet some of the six needs of mourning.

- An outside "room" can be equally effective. Do you have a porch or patio where you can just "be"? Locate a comfortable chair and install a tabletop fountain.

- Your sanctuary, even if just a simple room or nook, can become a place dedicated exclusively to the needs of the soul. The death of the person you love requires "soul work." Your creation of a sanctuary honors that reality.

CARPE DIEM
Identify a spot in your house that can be your sanctuary.
Begin readying it today.

71.

FIND A GRIEF "BUDDY"

*"Oh heck yeah, I'm still in contact with my peer mentor.
And she is the best thing (after my daughter) that happened to me
since my hubby got his wings. It's so nice to be able to talk to someone
who went through the same thing as me."*
— A surviving TAPS widow

- Though no one else will grieve this death just like you, there are often others who have had similar experiences. Among military families, you will likely be able to connect with others who have suffered the death of a loved one.

- Find a grief "buddy"—someone who is mourning a similar military death, perhaps someone from your loved one's unit, someone you can talk to, someone who also needs a companion in grief right now.

- TAPS offers a peer mentor program, which connects survivors one-on-one for companionship and support. Mentors are trained and at least a year beyond their own loss. You can talk with your peer mentor in person, over the phone, or by email—whatever works best for you. To learn more about the program or request a mentor, call 800-959-8277.

- Make a pact with your grief buddy to call each other whenever one of you needs to talk. Promise to listen without judgment. Commit to spending time together. You might arrange to meet once a week for breakfast or lunch with your grief buddy.

- Perhaps you've heard it said, "Friends are not a luxury, they are a necessity." This could never be more of a truth for you than right now.

CARPE DIEM

Do you know someone who also needs grief support right now?
Call and ask her out to lunch today. If it feels right, discuss the
possibility of being grief buddies.

72.

DON'T BE CAUGHT OFF GUARD BY "GRIEFBURSTS"

"It hurt because it mattered."
— John Green

- Sometimes heightened periods of sadness may overwhelm you. These times can seem to come of out nowhere and can be frightening and painful.

- Even long after the death, something as simple as a sound, a smell, or a phrase can bring on a "griefburst." You may see someone in a crowd who resembles the person who died. You may come across an old jacket or tennis racquet that belonged to the person who died. You may smell a certain food or cologne that reminds you of the person who died. These experiences tend to trigger sudden, unexpected, and powerful waves of emotion.

- For military survivors, these triggers can include the sight of a flag, the sound of a bugler playing "Taps," or the reverberation from a rifle volley, which they last heard at the funeral. Military uniforms, parades, and news coverage of military events can also set off a griefburst.

- Think of it this way: griefbursts may be how the person who has died says to you, "Don't forget me. Please don't forget me."

- Allow yourself to experience griefbursts without shame or self-judgment, no matter where and when they occur. If you would feel more comfortable, retreat to somewhere private when these strong feelings surface.

CARPE DIEM
Create an action plan for your next griefburst. For example,
you might plan to drop whatever you are doing and go for
a walk or record thoughts in your journal.

73.

VOLUNTEER

"If you want to lift yourself up, lift up someone else."
— Booker T. Washington

- Consider honoring the person who died by helping others in your community. Volunteer at a senior center, an elementary school, a local hospital—someplace that supports your values and feels close to your heart.

- Your loved one made the decision to serve. Think about honoring others who have made the same decision by volunteering to help homeless veterans or participating in a Veterans or Memorial Day event. Or volunteer with groups that honor our fallen heroes, like the Patriot Guard, the American Legion, or the TAPS Peer Mentor Program.

- What did your loved one love? What was he passionate about? Can you find a way to volunteer your time and talents to support the hobbies or causes that were important to him?

- If your schedule is too hectic, offer money instead of time. Make your donation in memory of the precious person who died.

CARPE DIEM

Call TAPS or your local VFW and ask for some suggestions about upcoming events you could participate in or organizations you could help.

74.

SPEND TIME IN "THIN PLACES"

"They hover as a cloud of witnesses above this Nation."
— Henry Ward Beecher

- In the Celtic tradition, "thin places" are spots where the separation between the physical world and the spiritual world seems tenuous. They are places where the veil between Heaven and Earth, between the holy and the everyday, are so thin that when we are near them, we intuitively sense the timeless, boundless spiritual world.

- There is a Celtic saying that heaven and earth are only three feet apart, but in the thin places that distance is even smaller.

- Thin places are usually outdoors, often where water and land meet or land and sky come together. You might find thin places on a riverbank, a beach, or a mountaintop.

- Go to a thin place to pray, to walk, or to simply sit in the presence of the holy.

CARPE DIEM

Your thin places are anywhere that fills you with awe and a sense of wonder. They are spots that refresh your spirit and make you feel closer to God. Go to a thin place today and sit in contemplative silence.

75.

ACCEPT THAT THERE MAY BE NO ANSWERS

"If there is a meaning in life at all, then there must be a meaning in suffering. Suffering is an ineradicable part of life, even as fate and death. Without suffering and death, human life cannot be complete."

— Viktor Frankl

- The fourth need of mourning is to search for meaning in life and death. This is the natural and necessary process of seeking to understand why such horrible things happen, why people have to die, why you and your family have been affected in this terrible way.

- Many military families believe that service to country is meaningful and find great pride and consolation in that. Others attribute meaning to service members' loyalty to their "band of brothers/sisters." If family members and friends do not agree with one another on this point, that's OK. Try to empathize with each others' points of view and be united instead by your love for the person who died and your need to support one another.

- Many people touched by traumatic loss come to realize that there may be no meaning to the tragedy itself. No rhyme or reason. No justice. But they also learn, over time, that there can be meaning in the ways they and others *respond* to what happened.

- What will I do now? How can I honor the life of the person who died? How can I become a more loving, compassionate, helpful person as a result of this tragedy? For many survivors, these are ultimately the questions that have answers. While you may not be at this place right now in your journey, our hope for you is that peace does indeed come to you.

CARPE DIEM

Deep in your soul, what is the most troubling question you have about the death? Take a walk today and give yourself some time to consider your question and why it haunts you. When you're ready, you may want to explore this question with someone you trust.

76.

WATCH THE SUN RISE

"May every sunrise hold more promise, every moonrise hold more peace."
— Unknown

- The sun is a powerful symbol of life and renewal. When was the last time you watched the sun rise? Do you remember being touched by its beauty and power?

- Think about our certainty that the sun shines elsewhere, even when we are in the darkness. Perhaps our loved ones are also "shining" elsewhere, even if we can't see them any longer.

- Plan an early morning breakfast or walk in a location where you can see the sun rise. Hike to the top of a hill. Have coffee next to a lake.

- Maybe you could make a sunrise ritual a tradition on your loved one's birthday or anniversary of the death.

CARPE DIEM

Invite a friend on an early morning drive. Choose a fitting destination for watching the sunrise. Pack a brunch of hot coffee, rolls, fresh fruit.

77.

LOOK FOR THE SURPRISES AND GIFTS IN YOUR DAY

"The most beautiful people we have known are those who have known defeat, known suffering, known struggle, known loss, and have found their way out of the depths. These persons have an appreciation, a sensitivity, and an understanding of life that fills them with compassion, gentleness, and a deep loving concern. Beautiful people do not just happen."
— Elisabeth Kübler-Ross

- Stop reading this and look around you where you are right this moment. Really try to look at the same things you see each day, but through a different set of eyes. What are you grateful for that is within your view? See it with awe. Look at the face of someone you love and rejoice that he is in your life.

- Whatever comes into your path today, consider it a gift. Take a moment to receive the gift and appreciate the giver. Embrace the warm feelings that come from being connected, from the link to gratefulness. Say "yes" and "thank you."

- Bill Keane, creator of the Family Circus comic strip, said, "Yesterday's the past, tomorrow's the future, but today is a gift. That's why it's called the present."

CARPE DIEM

Give someone else a small, unexpected gift today. It could simply be a phone call or a cup of coffee. It could be a smile. See what happens.

78.

LOOK INTO SUPPORT GROUPS

"A snowflake is one of God's most fragile creations,
but look what they can do when they stick together."
— Unknown

• Grief support groups are a healing, safe place for many mourners to express their thoughts and feelings.

• Support groups help mourners know that they're not alone. Members both support one another and learn from each other. And support groups often develop into very tight-knit, loyal, and lasting social circles.

• Sharing similar experiences with other mourners may help you feel like you're not alone, that you're not going crazy.

• If your loss was recent, you may not feel ready for a support group. Many mourners are more open to joining a support group six to nine months after the death.

CARPE DIEM
Click and call around today for support group information.
If you're feeling ready, plan to attend a meeting this week or next. If you need help finding an appropriate support group, call the TAPS National Military Survivor Helpline at 800-959-8277.

79.

CREATE A SHADOW BOX

"How lucky I am to have something that makes saying goodbye so hard."
— A. A. Milne

- A shadow box is a framed display case that hangs like a picture on the wall. Shadow boxes are for displaying collections or special mementos. Look through the items you've gathered in your loved one's memory box and see if you would like to display some of them in a shadow box.

- If you want to make a military-themed shadow box, gather up your loved one's medals, ribbons, citations, dog tags, and other mementos. Don't forget to feature a photo of your loved one in uniform in the display. Too often we forget the face behind the name on the headstone, and looking in their eyes can bring the military memorabilia to life.

- Go to your local hobby store and purchase a shadow box. (One with UV-protected glass will ensure that the shadow box contents won't fade.) On the display surface, arrange the mementos in a pleasing composition. Secure them with pins or tacks. Close the glass door and hang the shadow box on a wall where you'll get to see it often.

- If your loved one's battle buddies want to do something for your family, this could be a wonderful project for them. Creating the shadow box will also give them a chance to learn more about your service member and work through their own grief.

- Consider making a shadow box large enough to include your folded flag as part of the display. Placing it in the shadow box will give it a place of honor on your wall and ensure that it is protected and cherished forever.

CARPE DIEM
Buy an empty shadow box today.
Invite someone to help you with this project.

80.

SAY NO

"There are often many things we feel that we should do that, in fact, we don't really have to do. Getting to the point where we can tell the difference is a major milestone in the simplification process."
— Elaine St. James

- You may lack the energy as well as the desire to participate in activities you used to find pleasurable, especially soon after the death of someone you love. The fancy term for this is "anhedonia," which is the lack of ability to experience pleasure in things you previously found pleasurable. (Next time someone asks how you're doing, just say, "Oh, I'm feeling a bit anhedonistic today" and watch the response you get!)

- It's OK to say no when you're asked to help with a project, attend a party, or make a change you're not ready to make.

- When you say no, explain your feelings to the people who've invited you. Be sure to thank them for the invitation, but also be honest about your grief. Remember that expressing your grief outside of yourself— or mourning—is essential.

- Realize that you can't keep saying no forever. There will always be that first family reunion, birthday party, holiday dinner, etc. Don't miss out on life's most joyful celebrations.

CARPE DIEM
Say no to something today. Allow yourself not to feel guilty about it.

81.

WATCH FOR WARNING SIGNS

"When you're at peace with yourself and you love yourself, it's virtually impossible for you to do things to yourself that are destructive."
— Wayne Dyer

- Sometimes mourners fall back on self-destructive behaviors to get through this difficult time.

- Try to be honest with yourself about drug or alcohol use. Long after the death, are you still taking drugs—prescription or otherwise—to make it through the day? Are you drinking in an attempt to dull the pain? If you're in over your head, ask someone for help.

- Keep in mind that a traumatic loss can actually change the biochemistry of your brain. You may very appropriately be taking prescribed antidepressant, anti-anxiety, or sleeping medications right now. And if you were taking medications before the death, you should continue doing so under your doctor's supervision. If you're forgetting to take your medication, ask someone to help you remember.

- Are you having suicidal thoughts or feelings? Please, talk to someone today. The National Suicide Prevention Lifeline is available 24/7, 365, and offers assistance in both English and Spanish: 800-273-8255.

CARPE DIEM
Acknowledging to ourselves that we have a problem may come too late.
If someone suggests that you need help, consider yourself lucky
to be so well-loved and get help.

82.

RELEASE ANY AMBIVALENCE OR REGRETS YOU MAY HAVE ABOUT THE FUNERAL AND BURIAL

"Do the best you can. When you know better, do better."
— Maya Angelou

- Funerals are a wonderful means of expressing our beliefs, thoughts, and feelings about the life and death of those we love. Funerals help us acknowledge the reality of the death, give testimony to the life of the person who died, express our grief, support each other, and embrace our faith and beliefs about life and death.

- Yet for many survivors of sudden death, funeral planning is difficult. Funeral and burial decisions may have been made quickly, while you were still in deep shock and disbelief. Sometimes some of these decisions seem less than ideal with the benefit of hindsight.

- If you harbor any negative feelings about the funeral or memorial service, know this: you and everyone else who was a part of the service did the best they could do at the time. You cannot change what happened, but you can talk about what happened and share your thoughts and feelings with someone who cares.

- On the other hand, many families who had a personalized, meaningful funeral are forever comforted by their memories of the ceremony. If your loved one's burial included military honors, you experienced something sacred in American tradition. Did you know that the words to the bugle call "Taps," often played at the end of a military burial, are actually a prayer? "Day is done. Gone the sun, from the lake from the hills, from the sky. All is well. Safely rest. God is nigh."

- It's never too late to hold another memorial service. Perhaps a tree-planting ceremony or a small gathering on the anniversary of the death could be a forum for sharing memories and prayer.

CARPE DIEM
If you harbor regrets or anger about the funeral and burial, talk about these feelings with someone today. Perhaps the two of you together can create an "action plan" to help make things better.

83.

SEEK SUPPORT ON ANNIVERSARIES

"Death leaves a heartache no one can heal.
Love leaves a memory no one can steal."
— From a headstone in Ireland

• Anniversaries—of the death, life events, birthdays, Memorial Day, Veterans Day—can be especially hard when you are grieving.

• The anniversary of the death is often especially painful. Thoughts about how the person died may resurface. Anger at those responsible or the circumstances might boil again. Fear and anxiety often heighten.

• These are times you may want to plan ahead for. The anniversary of the death may be a good day to plan a small memorial service at the cemetery or scattering site. Ritualizing your thoughts and feelings through prayer, song, and memory sharing with others will help create supportive, healing structure on this day.

• Reach out to others on birthdays and other anniversaries. Talk about your feelings with a close friend.

CARPE DIEM
What's the next anniversary you've been anticipating?
Make a plan right now for what you will do on that day.
Enlist a friend's help so you won't be alone.

84.

SCHEDULE SOMETHING THAT GIVES YOU PLEASURE EACH AND EVERY DAY

"Sorrow enlarges the capacity of the heart for joy."
— Richard Mahew

- When we're in mourning, often we need something to look forward to, a reason to get out of bed today.

- It's hard to look forward to each day when you know you will be experiencing pain and sadness.

- To counterbalance your normal and necessary mourning, plan something you enjoy doing every day. Reading, baking, going for a walk, having lunch with a friend, playing computer games—whatever brings you enjoyment.

- If you can, try reserving the hour before bed for the simple pleasures you enjoy best, such as one glass of wine, your favorite TV show, texting with your friends, reading a good book, or eating a special snack.

- Another tactic you might try is setting a reminder on your phone to do something that makes you smile.

CARPE DIEM
What's on tap for today? Squeeze in something you enjoy,
no matter how hectic your schedule.

85.

CAPTURE YOUR LOVED ONE'S STORY

"Although setbacks of all kinds may discourage us, the grand,
old process of storytelling puts us in touch with strengths we may
have forgotten, with wisdom that has faded or disappeared,
and with hopes that have fallen into darkness."
— Nancy Mellon

• You probably—and understandably—feel that your loved one's story was cut short. Most people who die a military death are healthy and young.

• Yet this precious person was privileged to live a singular, never-to-be-repeated life. She was born, she lived, she loved you and many others. She joined the military. She did and saw and enjoyed many things. She made a difference. She tragically died.

• One way to honor your loved one's death is to capture his life. There's so much more to know and say than could ever be included in an obituary or eulogy. What if you undertook a project to write your loved one's story and self-publish it in book form?

• You could write your loved one's biography yourself by interviewing people who knew him in various parts of his life, such as elementary school, his first job, church or Boy Scouts, boot camp, officer school, etc. Or you could invite a number of people to contribute a "chapter."

• Add photos, captions, passages from favorite books or songs, favorite sayings and lists of favorite foods, movies, games, sports teams, etc.

• What a special keepsake such a book would make for your family, now and generations into the future.

CARPE DIEM

Don't forget to record your loved one's story in the Library of Congress' Veterans History Project: www.loc.gov/vets/.

86.

TALK TO A COUNSELOR

"There are many ways of getting strong. Sometimes talking is the best way."
— Andre Agassi

- While grief counseling is not for everyone, many mourners are helped through their grief journeys by a compassionate counselor. Survivors of sudden, violent death may also be helped with traumatic grief issues.

- If possible, find a counselor who has experience with grief and loss. A counselor experienced with trauma loss and PTSD is even better.

- The VA offers free grief counseling to parents, siblings, spouses, and children of Armed Forces personnel who died in service of their country. Family of reservists and National Guardsmen who die on duty are also eligible. If your loved one was not on active duty at the time of death, TAPS can connect you with an experienced trauma counselor near you. Some provide free services to military personnel and families through the Give an Hour program. Visit www.taps.org for more information.

- Your church pastor may also be a good person to talk to during this time, but only if she affirms your need to mourn this death and search for meaning.

- If you have children, family counseling sessions may also be beneficial. Sometimes this is the only way to share difficult stories and hear one another talk about painful thoughts and feelings.

CARPE DIEM
Call the VA at 202-461-6530 or TAPS at 800-959-8277
to learn more about counseling benefits and options.

87.

TAKE A MINI-VACATION

"Travel is the only thing you buy that makes you richer."
— Unknown

- Always keep in mind that when you're grieving, good self-care is essential not only to your survival but also to your long-term healing.

- Don't have time to take time off? Plan several mini-vacations this month instead.

- What creative ideas can you come up with to renew yourself? Here are a few ideas to get you started:

  - Have a spiritual growth weekend. Retreat into nature. Plan some alone time.
  - Go for a drive with no particular destination in mind. Explore the countryside, slow down, and observe what you see.
  - Treat yourself to a night in a hotel or bed and breakfast.
  - Visit a museum or a zoo.
  - Go to a yard sale or auction.
  - Go rollerskating or rollerblading with a friend.
  - Drop by a health-food store and walk the aisles.
  - Schedule a massage with a professional massage therapist.

CARPE DIEM
Plan a mini-vacation for today. Spend one hour doing something special.

88.

PAY ATTENTION TO SYNCHRONICITIES

"Coincidence is God's way of being anonymous."
— Laura Pedersen

- Stuff happens, the saying goes. (Well, you know the real saying, but this is a respectful book. ☺)

- The philosophy embedded in that aphorism is that things happen over which you have no control, and you need to resign yourself to the fact that life is unpredictable and often bad.

- Sometimes life is bad. Sometimes stuff happens. But often, if you are paying attention, if you are living on purpose, stuff happens that is nothing short of miraculous.

- At night you dream of a friend you haven't seen for years, and the next day she calls you, out of the blue. You hear a song on the car radio that perfectly captures what you're feeling that moment. Your furnace breaks down and you receive an unexpected check in the mail.

- You might also experience synchronicities that seem to be messages from the person who died. This is normal and natural, and if you find comfort and meaning in them, rejoice.

- Pay attention to coincidences. Believe that they may be telling you something—even guiding you. As the Dalai Lama said, "I am open to the guidance of synchronicity and do not let expectations hinder my path."

CARPE DIEM

The next time you experience what feels like a coincidence,
mark it on your calendar or write about it in your journal.
Contemplate what guidance it may be offering.

89.

THINK POSITIVE

*"Each night I put my head to my pillow, I try to tell myself
I'm strong because I've gone one more day without you."*
— Unknown

- After a traumatic death, it's normal—even necessary—to feel numb, depressed, afraid, angry, and many other difficult feelings. The world has become a scary place, and someone you love has been taken from you.

- Indeed, you must allow yourself ample time to acknowledge and experience your painful thoughts and feelings. Life will be hard for a while.

- But over time and with the love and support of others, your life can be happy again. You must trust in your ability to heal. You must trust that you will live and love fully again.

- Even in the midst of your grief, strive to think positive. Neuroscientists now understand that the human brain has the power to create its own reality. If you believe—really believe—that you can do something, you probably can.

- Visualize yourself nurturing a friendship or achieving a goal. Visualize yourself laughing and having fun. Visualize yourself at peace. You may not be able to live these realities today, but projecting yourself forward into a happier future may well help you achieve that future.

CARPE DIEM

The death is in the past. You cannot change that, but you can affect the future. What is most worrying you about the coming days or weeks? Close your eyes and visualize a positive outcome to the situation.

90.

GIVE YOURSELF A PUSH

"If it doesn't challenge you, it doesn't change you."
— Unknown

- Your military loved one was probably a doer. That's something the military trains into people.

- People who serve in the military have to learn to push themselves. They get fitter than they'd ever been. They take on challenges that they never imagined they could. They dig deep and find reserves of courage and strength inside them.

- Even as you are being gentle, compassionate, and patient with yourself—all of which you very much need and deserve—you can also, now and then, give yourself a push.

- If you've been avoiding or repressing some part of your grief for too long, dig deep and find the courage to look it square in the face and express it.

- Remember your loved one's courage and find your own. Trust us—it's there.

CARPE DIEM
Is there something you've been avoiding that you know you
really need to do in order to fully and honestly embrace
and express your grief? Today's the day.

91.

DRAW A "GRIEF MAP"

"Deep grief sometimes is almost like a specific location, a coordinate on a map of time. When you are standing in that forest of sorrow, you cannot imagine that you could ever find your way to a better place. But if someone can assure you that they themselves have stood in that same place, and now have moved on, sometimes this will bring hope."
— Elizabeth Gilbert

- The death of your loved one may have stirred up all kinds of thoughts and feelings inside you. These thoughts and feelings may seem overwhelming or even "crazy."

- Rest assured that you're not crazy—you're grieving. Your thoughts and feelings—no matter how scary or strange they seem to you—are normal and necessary.

- Sometimes, corralling all your varied thoughts and feelings in one place can make them feel more manageable. You could write about them, but you can also draw them out in diagram form.

- Make a large circle at the center of your map and label it GRIEF. This circle represents your thoughts and feeling since the death. Now draw lines radiating out of this circle and label each line with a thought or feeling that has contributed to your grief. For example, you might write GUILT in a bubble at the end of one line. Next to the word guilt, jot down notes about why you feel guilty.

- Your grief map needn't look pretty or follow any certain rules. The most important thing is the process of creating it. When you're finished, explain it to someone who cares about you.

CARPE DIEM

Stop by your local art supply or hobby shop today and pick up a large piece of poster board or banner paper. Set aside an hour or so to work on your grief map today.

92.

LIVE FOR BOTH OF YOU

"The legacy of heroes is the memory of a great name and the inheritance of a great example."
— Benjamin Disraeli

- Someone you love has died, and you are alive. Even though you are grieving and in pain, your life here on Earth continues. Life does indeed, as they say, go on.

- We understand that it can be hard to keep going after the death of a special loved one. But think of it this way: You have a wondrous opportunity to live and love fully from this moment forward. Has this death made you more aware of the preciousness of our own life?

- You can choose not just to survive but to truly live in honor and memory of the person who died. Find ways to celebrate his life, even as you richly live your own.

- In his honor and memory, be the best version of "you" that you can be.

CARPE DIEM
Finish something your loved one started.

93.

EXPRESS YOUR GRATITUDE

*"Nothing new can come into your life unless you are
grateful for what you already have."*
Michael Bernard

- Despite the tragedy, you are probably, underneath the hurt, grateful for many things in your life. When you feel mired in painful, sad feelings, try making a list of that for which you are grateful.

- You may be grateful for your children or partner. For your siblings. For your parents. For your friends. You may be grateful for your job or your education. You might also try naming the little things that make you feel grateful: the way the sun danced on your countertop this morning; the peace you felt after going for a walk; the song you just heard on the radio.

- Don't forget to express your gratitude to those who offered help and comfort at the time of the death. Military personnel, battle buddies, medical workers, friends, even complete strangers may have gone above and beyond the call of duty to help you or someone in your family.

- Sometimes it helps to express your gratitude to the person who died. Write her a letter telling her what she meant to you and the lessons you learned from her. Tell her how grateful you are that her life, though too short, was joined with yours.

CARPE DIEM
Today, call or text someone you're grateful for and tell them thank you.

94.

BELIEVE IN YOUR CAPACITY TO HEAL

"Believe you can and you're halfway there."
— Theodore Roosevelt

• All the traumatized grievers we have ever had the privilege of meeting and learning from would want us to tell you this: you will survive.

• If your loss was recent, it may feel as if you cannot get through this. You can and you will. It will probably be excruciatingly difficult, yes, but over time and with the love and support of others, your grief will soften and you will find ways to be happy again. There will come a day when the death is not the first thing you think of when you wake up in the morning.

• Many people who suffer a traumatic loss also struggle with feeling they don't *want* to survive. Again, longtime traumatized grievers want you to know that while this feeling is normal, it will pass. One day in the not-too-distant future, you will feel that life is worth living again. For now, think of how important you are to your children, your parents and siblings, your friends.

• As time passes, you may also choose not simply to survive, but to truly live. The remainder of your life can be full and rich and satisfying if you choose life over mere existence.

CARPE DIEM

If you're feeling you won't make it through the next few weeks or months, talk to someone about your feelings of panic and despair. The simple act of expressing these feelings may render them a little less powerful.

95.

SEEK YOUR HIGHER SELF

*"Grief and love are conjoined; you don't get one without the other.
All I can do is love her, and love the world, emulate her by
living with daring and spirit and joy."*
— Jandy Nelson

- We often say that those who serve in the military are serving a higher purpose. What is your higher purpose?

- When you "live" in the realm of the Higher Self, you befriend divine qualities that are within you, such as, caring, joy, strength, appreciation, and love. The Higher Self is the spiritual, and some believe immortal, part of who you are. While the Higher Self recognizes that grief, loss, and sadness are part of the journey, it also realizes you can survive and slowly discover renewed meaning and purpose in your life.

- The Higher Self knows that all situations in life—happy and sad—can be used as springboards for learning and growth. It doesn't see the outside world as a threat; it sees it as a place to contribute and be hopeful about the future. Your Higher Self holds wisdom beyond your wildest dreams. This amazing wisdom can lead you into and through the wilderness of your grief. The Higher Self believes that out of the dark comes light, but that you must also descend into grief before you transcend.

- In moments of despair, look for ways to connect to your Higher Self. Also remember your loved one's Higher Self and try to emulate her best qualities.

CARPE DIEM
Remind yourself today to try to aspire to your Higher Self.

96.

TEACH OTHERS ABOUT GRIEF
AND MOURNING

*"The fact that I can plant a seed and it becomes a flower, share a bit
of knowledge and it becomes another's, smile at someone and receive
a smile in return, are to me continual spiritual exercises."*
— Leo Buscaglia

- To love is to one day mourn. You have learned this most poignant of life's lessons.

- Maybe you could teach what you are learning to others. Tell your friends and family about the six needs of mourning. Teach them how they can best support you. Also teach them about the misconceptions of mourning (Idea 24).

- Share your wisdom in the safety of a grief support group.

- Remember that each person's grief is unique. Your experiences will not be shared or appreciated by everyone.

CARPE DIEM
What is the one most helpful thing you've learned about grief and mourning? Share this hard-won understanding with someone today.

97.

IMAGINE YOUR REUNION WITH THE PERSON WHO DIED

*"What matters most is what I leave behind for you to keep.
So smile when you think of me. Like we blinked, not a moment is gone.
We'll pick up where we left off."*

— Unknown

- Most mourners we've talked to—and that number runs into the tens of thousands—are comforted by a belief or a hope that somehow, somewhere, the person who died lives on in health and happiness. For some, this belief is grounded in religious faith and the afterlife. For others it is simply a spiritual sense.

- Service members often talk about Valhalla instead of Heaven. Many believe in the idea, taken from Norse mythology, that fallen warriors gather in a heavenly hall to celebrate.

- If you believe in Heaven or Valhalla, close your eyes and imagine what it might be like. Imagine the person who died strong and smiling. Imagine him doing what he enjoyed most in the company of loved ones who have gone before him.

- Here on Earth, some mourners have dreams in which the person who died seems to be communicating with them. Some feel the overwhelming presence of their loved one on occasion. Some actually "see" or "hear" the person. These are common, normal experiences and are often quite comforting.

CARPE DIEM
If you believe in Heaven or an afterlife (or even if you're not sure),
imagine the reunion you may one day have with the person who died.
Imagine the joy of being able to see, touch, and talk to this person again.
Imagine what you will say to one another.

98.
UNDERSTAND THE CONCEPT OF "RECONCILIATION"

"What happens when people open their hearts? They get better."
— Haruki Murakami

- Sometimes you'll hear about mourners "recovering" from grief. This term is damaging because it implies that grief is an illness that must be cured. It also connotes a return to the way things were before the death.

- Mourners don't recover from grief. We become "reconciled" to it. In other words, we learn to live with it and are forever changed by it.

- This does not mean a life of misery, however. Mourners often not only heal but grow through grief. Our lives can potentially be deeper and more meaningful after the death of someone loved.

- Reconciliation takes time. You may not become truly reconciled to your loss for several years and even then will have "griefbursts" (see Idea 72) forever.

- We believe every human being wants to "mourn well" the deaths of those they love. It is as essential as breathing. Some people make the choice to give momentum to their mourning, while others deny or avoid it. The path you choose to take will make all the difference. Move toward your grief and go on to live until you die!

CARPE DIEM
Write down the following definition of reconciliation and post it somewhere you will see it often: I am learning to integrate my grief into my life. I will not "get over" my grief, but if I do the necessary work of mourning, I will go on to live a full life, one with meaning and joy.

99.

CHOOSE TO LIVE

"Don't live the same year 75 times and call it a life."
— Robin Sharma

- Sudden, violent death often leaves mourners feeling powerless. You were powerless to prevent the death, and you're powerless to reverse it. But you can regain a feeling of power by deciding to take control of the rest of your life.

- Will you merely exist for the remainder of your days, or will you choose to truly live?

- Many mourners take up a new life direction after an unexpected death. Has the death given you a new perspective on life? How can you choose to act on this new perspective?

- What did the person who died love in life? How can you help nurture that love in the world in an ongoing, positive way?

- Sometimes choosing to live simply means living mindfully, with an appreciation for all that is good and beautiful and with a deep, abiding kindness to others.

- As a wise person once observed, "When old words die out on the tongue, new melodies spring forth from the heart."

CARPE DIEM
Do one small thing today that demonstrates your desire to live over merely existing.

100.

STRIVE TO GROW THROUGH GRIEF

*"Someone who has experienced trauma also has gifts to offer all of us—
in their depth, their knowledge of universal vulnerability,
and their experience of the power of compassion."*

— Sharon Salzberg

- Over time, you may find that you are growing emotionally and spiritually as a result of your grief journey. I understand that you've paid a high price for this growth and that you would gladly trade it for one more minute with the person who died. Still, the death may have brought bittersweet gifts into your life that you would not otherwise have.

- Many people emerge from the early years of traumatic grief as stronger, more capable people. You may find that you're more assertive and apt to say what you really believe and be who you really are. You may no longer put up with baloney. You've already survived the worst life has to offer, so anything still to come can't be so bad. And you've learned what's truly important and what's not.

- What's more, many of you will discover depths of compassion for others that you never knew you had. Many survivors of traumatic loss grow to volunteer, undertake daily kindnesses, become more emotionally and spiritually tuned-in to others and more interpersonally effective.

CARPE DIEM
Consider the ways in which you may be "growing through grief."

A FINAL WORD FROM BONNIE

Our loved ones' lives and their legacies of service are woven into the fabric of who we are now, and who we will become. They will continue to teach us lessons, inspire us to do better, and remind us how truly precious life is. Death may end a physical life, but it does not end a relationship. We will redefine who they forever are to us, and they will remain with us always.

I was once asked, "If you had known the intense pain of this grief, would you rather have never known him?" I was shaken at the thought of that. I would never have sacrificed a moment of the time we had together. I just wanted more! And then it occurred to me, no matter when we lose those we love, it would never have been enough! But I thank God for the little while we did have with them. They lived, and we loved them, and that love will continue.

The theme of TAPS is "Remember the love. Celebrate the life. Share the journey." Over the years, there came a time when I woke up first with gratitude, remembering that he lived and we found love, before feeling the pain that he died. It was a quiet shift that took place in tiny movements, some forward, many backward, and it was a journey to a place of peace.

TAPS is America's family for all whose loved ones' lives included selfless service to our nation. Our loved ones aren't defined by the geography or circumstance of their deaths; they are forever remembered by the way in which they lived. We come together now to share this journey, and in doing so, ease our pain in the knowledge we are not alone. We are forever bonded by the life and the love. And the power of that community gently mends our broken hearts.

A FINAL WORD FROM ALAN

I hope you have found this book a source of compassionate guidance and support. Keep it handy. Whenever you find yourself struggling with your grief, I encourage you to get it out again and see if you can find a bit of encouragement and hope in its pages.

I also encourage you to contact and stay in touch with TAPS. They are an excellent organization made up of fellow travelers who have not only suffered a military death but who understand the necessity of grief and mourning. Many of their staff members have trained at my Center for Loss and Life Transition. During my longtime relationship with TAPS, I have seen the good they do and the passion with which they do it. Not many grievers have access to the depth and breadth of compassionate services they provide, but you do. I hope you will remember your needs of mourning and reach out for and accept their help. Over time, they can help you relight your divine spark and find joy and continued meaning in life.

Godspeed.

RESOURCES

Arlington National Cemetery
877-907-8585 | www.arlingtoncemetery.mil
If you wish to have your loved one buried or interred at Arlington
National Cemetery, ask your local funeral home to telephone the inter-
ment office and arrange for the service.

Department of Veterans Affairs
www.va.gov
The VA offers free bereavement counseling at community-based Vet
Centers throughout the U.S. For details, call the Bereavement Counseling
Service at 202-461-6530.

Gold Star Mothers, Inc.
202-265-0991 | www.goldstarmoms.com
Gold Star Mothers is a congressionally chartered nonprofit organization of
mothers who lost a son or daughter in the service of our country.

Gold Star Wives of America, Inc.
888-751-6350 | www.goldstarwives.org
Gold Star Wives is a congressionally chartered nonprofit service organization that provides services to active-duty and service-connected military
widows and widowers.

Military One Source
800-342-9647 | www.militaryonesource.mil
Military One Source is a confidential Department of Defense-funded
program providing comprehensive, free information on every aspect of
military life.

National Military Family Association
703-931-6632 | www.militaryfamily.org
The goal of the NMFA is to educate military families about the rights, benefits, and services available to them, and to promote and protect the interests of military families by influencing the development and implementation of legislation and policies affecting them.

Society of Military Widows
800-842-3451, ext. 1003 | www.militarywidows.org
The Society of Military Widows is a nonprofit organization that serves the interests of women whose husbands died while on active military duty, of service-connected illness, or during disability or regular retirement from the military services.

Tragedy Assistance Program for Survivors (TAPS)
800-959-TAPS (8277) | www.taps.org
The Tragedy Assistance Program for Survivors provides comfort and care for all those grieving the loss of a loved one who died while serving in the Armed Forces, regardless of their relationship to the deceased or the circumstances of the death. TAPS provides comfort and care through comprehensive services and programs including peer-based emotional support, casework assistance, connections to community-based care, the 24/7 National Military Survivor Helpline, regional and national survivor seminars, retreats and camps, and grief and trauma resources.

USO
302-423-6368 | www.uso.org/families-of-the-fallen-support
The USO Families of the Fallen Support Program provides travel support, respite, and comfort to families who are traveling through airports across the United States. The USO works with airline and airport security officials to expedite the check-in process for families of the fallen traveling to Dover Air Force Base, connects family members arriving from multiple locations and arranges for accommodations if a family's flight is missed or delayed, coordinates with each military branch to link families with ground transportation to and from Dover Air Force Base, supports military escorts who accompany their fallen comrades to their final homecoming, and assists families traveling to and from memorial services when requested.

TRAINING AND SPEAKING ENGAGEMENTS

To contact Dr. Wolfelt about speaking engagements or
training opportunities at his Center for Loss and Life Transition,
email him at DrWolfelt@centerforloss.com.

ALSO BY ALAN WOLFELT

The Depression of Grief

COPING WITH YOUR SADNESS AND KNOWING
WHEN TO GET HELP

When someone you love dies, it's normal and necessary
to grieve. Grief is the thoughts and feelings you have
inside you, and sadness is often the most prominent
and painful emotion. In other words, it's normal to be
depressed after a loss. This compassionate guide will
help you understand your natural depression, express it
in ways that will help you heal, and know when you may
be experiencing a more severe or clinical depression that
would be eased by professional treatment. A section for caregivers that explores the
new DSM-5 criteria for Major Depression is also included.

ISBN 978-1-61722-193-4 • 128 pages • softcover • $14.95

"This enlightening book revealed to me that I am not flawed
and it further gave me the strength to go back and do a bit
more work so I could truly mourn the loss of my mom
and start living life once again." — Kerry Bratton

All Dr. Wolfelt's publications can be ordered by mail from:
Companion Press
3735 Broken Bow Road I Fort Collins, Colorado 80526
Phone: (970) 226-6050 I www.centerforloss.com